MYSTERIES OF THE MODERN WORLD

MYSTERIES OF THE MODERN WORLD

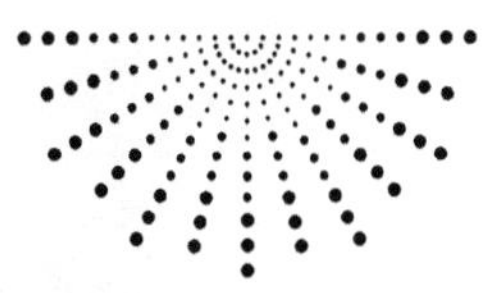

E.B. WHEELER

ISBN: 978-1-960033-15-4

First printing: November 2024

Published by Rowan Ridge Press, Utah

Cover image via Deposit Photos

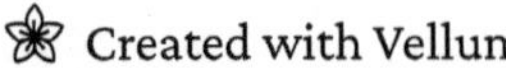

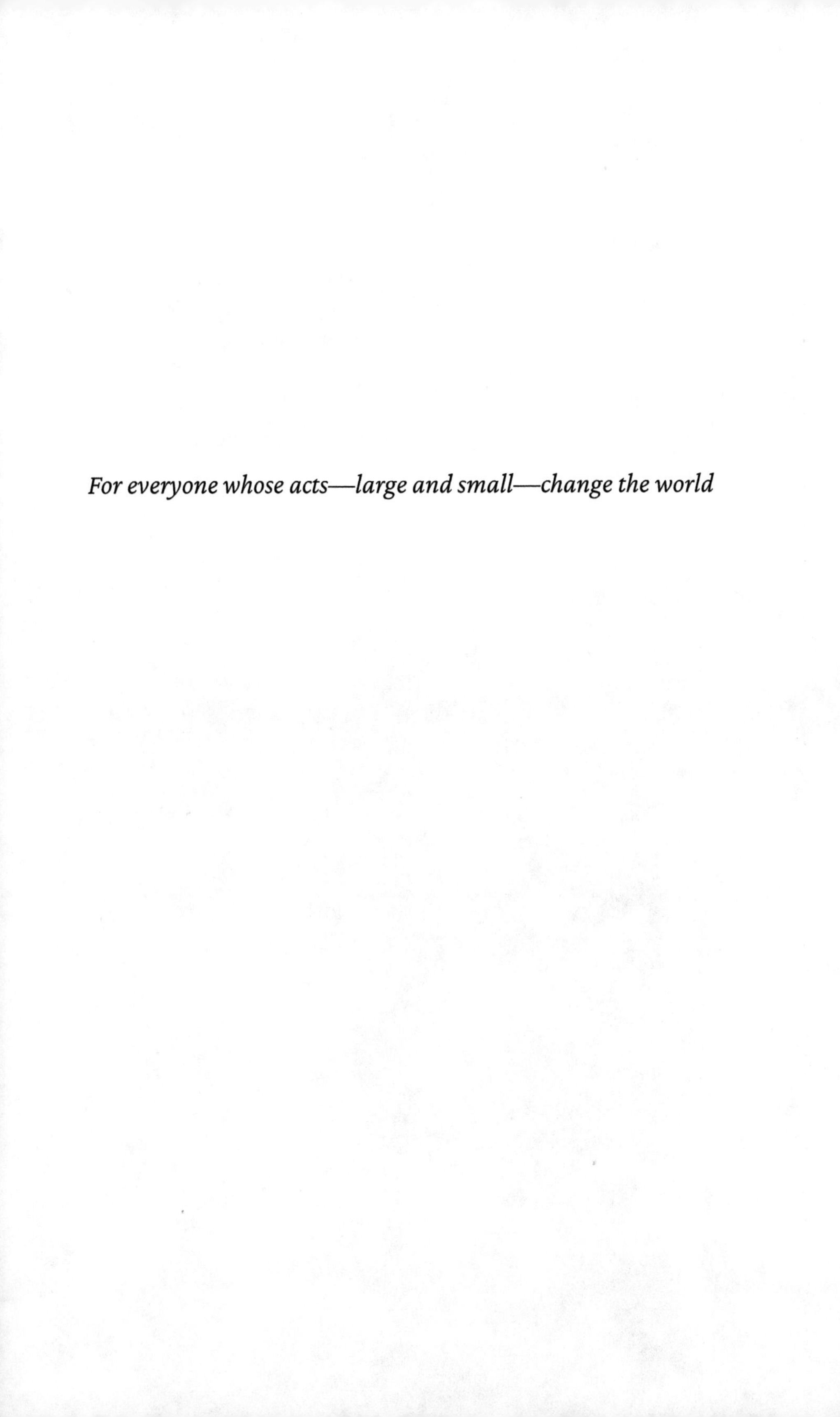

For everyone whose acts—large and small—change the world

NOTE FROM THE AUTHOR

The stories in this book are true, based on the most reliable sources I could find (you can see a list of the main sources for each chapter at the back of the book). Writing about history is always tricky because people record what they think happened, or what they remember or heard about, but no one has all the answers. Two people can remember the same event very differently. Even with more recent history like the mysteries in this book where some of the witnesses might still be alive, they don't always agree about what they saw or heard. Sometimes, they don't bother writing down important details because they assume "everyone knows that" or "what I think doesn't matter." Occasionally, they lie or make things up! History sleuths have to put the truth together like a puzzle, but we often don't have all the pieces or can't see how they fit. That can make historical mysteries more interesting to try to solve.

Where possible, I used first-hand accounts to reconstruct

these stories, but I sometimes had to guess exactly what people said, did, and thought based on the information available. I have done my best to be accurate, but real people are too complex to fit on a page, and I apologize if I misrepresented anyone

I hope you enjoy trying to solve each mystery and perhaps find one that sparks your curiosity to dive deeper into the mysteries of history.

DYATLOV PASS,
RUSSIA
LAKE BAIKAL,
RUSSIA
BELGIUM
NORTH
ATLANTIC
POLAND
AREA 51,
USA
CHINA
EGYPT
LAOS
HOWLAND ISLAND,
PACIFIC OCEAN
AUSTRALIA
SOUTH AFRICA
ARGENTINA

CHAPTER ONE

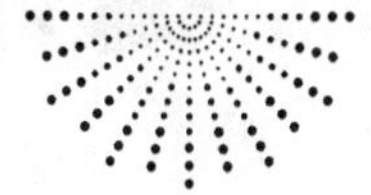

The Vanished Ship

On a frigid April night in 1912, the unimaginable happened: The "practically unsinkable" *Titanic* hit an iceberg four days into its first voyage and began tilting into the icy waters of the North Atlantic. Crew and passengers, woken from sleep, gathered on the decks. They bundled into coats and blankets against the biting cold of the night air and strapped on life preservers. The crew loaded women and children into lifeboats as a precaution, and the ship's band played popular music to keep passengers calm.

Most passengers weren't afraid yet. They trusted in the promise of the "practically unsinkable" *Titanic.*

The Titanic, pictured here, was a modern marvel in 1912. Image by Francis Godolphin Osbourne Stuart courtesy of Wikimedia.

The *Titanic* represented the early twentieth century's belief that science and progress knew no limits. Through science, many trusted that all of humanity's problems could be solved, and people could even conquer nature. At the time, the *Titanic* was the largest ship ever to sail, twenty-five stories tall, as long as four city blocks, weighing 52,000 tons (as much as 260 modern commercial airplanes), but designed like a luxury hotel with four elevators and the first swimming pool built on board a ship.

Its hull was divided into sixteen watertight compartments, so if one filled with water, it could be sealed off, and the others would still hold air and keep the *Titanic* afloat. Because of its size, it wasn't the fastest ship, but it was able to go 23 knots (26 miles or 42 kilometers per hour), a respectable speed for the time.

This picture of Titanic's *"sister ship"* Olympic *shows the size of these ships. Notice how small the man at the bottom looks compared the ship's enormous rudder. Image courtesy of Wikimedia.*

On the terrible night of the accident, the *Titanic* was moving close to its top speed through the moonless dark. The air was so cold, the water so still, and the night so black that it played tricks on people's eyes, similar to mirages in the desert.

Second Officer Charles Lightoller, in a 1936 interview, remembered it as, "Not a breath of wind and the sea like a sheet of glass."

When the lookouts finally spotted the iceberg less than a mile away, the *Titanic* couldn't simply stop or turn to avoid collision. Imagine trying to steer an entire small town moving at twenty miles per hour. Yet they managed to veer so the ship didn't hit the ice head-on. The *Titanic* scraped along the iceberg.

Lightoller, in the US Senate inquiry into the disaster, said the impact brought only, "A slight jar and a grinding sound."

Fourth officer Joseph Boxhall, in the same Senate inquiry, recalled that the iceberg "... seemed to me to be just a small black mass not rising very high out of the water..."

But the impact punctured the hull and spilled water into six of the waterproof compartments, all on the same side of the ship. This made the ship tilt. The engineers hadn't considered this possibility, so the watertight walls didn't go far above the waterline. As the ship tilted, the water overflowed and poured from one compartment to another, making the ship lurch farther into the sea. The "unsinkable" ship was going under, whether the passengers and crew believed it or not.

Naval laws of the time didn't require enough lifeboats for the more than 2,000 passengers on the ship—people believed that a ship like the *Titanic* would sink slowly, so the boats were meant to take passengers to a rescue ship and then return for more. With too few lifeboats for everyone, the priority was on boarding women and children—especially those from the first class section of the ship—who were considered less likely to survive waiting out the cold.

Lightoller, in his 1936 interview, said, "I told them it was merely a precaution and that very likely they'd all be taken on board again at daylight or at the worst taken on board the ship everyone could clearly see only a few miles away. We could see all her lights quite plainly."

When asked why he didn't pack the first lifeboats full, Lightoller told the US Congressional inquiry, "I did not know it was urgent then. I had no idea it was urgent."

Second Officer Charles Lightoller went down with the Titanic *after helping to load lifeboats. He survived the sinking along with several other men by climbing onto an overturned lifeboat that had been washed overboard in the sinking. As the highest ranking officer to survive, his testimony was especially valuable in later inquiries into the disaster. Image courtesy of Wikimedia.*

The rest of the passengers had to stay warm and dry as long as possible, clinging to the *Titanic* until help arrived. If they plunged into the black, icy waters, only 28 degrees Fahrenheit (-2 Celsius), their lives would be counted in minutes.

Meanwhile, Fourth Officer Boxhall told the Senate inquiry, "My attention until the time I left the ship was mostly taken up with firing off distress rockets and trying to signal a steamer that was almost ahead of us... By the way she was heading she seemed to be meeting us... She got close enough, as I thought, to read our electric Morse signal, and I signaled to her; I told her to come at once, we were sinking... I can not say I saw any reply... I would signal with the Morse and then go ahead and send off a rocket, and then go back and have a look at the ship, until I was finally sent away."

Other crew and passengers on the deck of the *Titanic* also looked to the lights of that other ship glowing across the darkness, maybe five miles (eight kilometers) in the distance. Certainly, that ship would have received their distress calls on the radio and in Morse code or would notice the flares Boxhall blasted into the air like fireworks. Perhaps it could even hear the shouts of crew members directing passengers or the notes of the band's violins.

But as lifeboats set off into the arctic darkness, the other ship kept its distance. When the *Titanic* filled with water and its front dipped down into the ocean, the passengers' hope turned to dread. The *Titanic*'s stern (back end) lifted into the cold night sky until the bitter cold and weaknesses in the metal broke the ship in half. The front half sank. The back end dropped back into the inky black ocean and then went under. The last passengers jumped or were pulled into the sea.

As those passengers hit the ice-cold water, the freezing temperature stole their breath. Some were knocked unconscious and drowned almost immediately. Others fought for the surface, the cold making their muscles stiff and their minds slow. A few made it to the lifeboats. Others treaded water, relying on their life vests to keep them afloat and hoping for rescue to arrive. After all, it went against the laws of the sea and of humanity to leave shipwrecked crew and passengers to a dark, icy death.

Yet within minutes, the people in the water grew silent and still, lost to hypothermia. Only those in the lifeboats remained alive, the cold air biting their faces and hands and seeping through wet clothing.

Titanic *survivors on a lifeboat, as photographed by* Carpathia *passenger J.W. Barker. Image courtesy of the National Archives and Wikimedia.*

For an hour and a half, the survivors huddled in the lifeboats, surrounded by the dead in the stillness and the dark and praying for rescue. It finally came in the form of the *Carpathia*. The passenger steamship, guided by Captain Arthur Rostrun, had been 58 miles away when it picked up the Titanic's first distress call.

Rostrun was hours from the *Titanic* under normal conditions, but he immediately ordered, "Turn this ship around."

Rostrun assumed a closer ship would reach the *Titanic* first, but there were people in danger on the waters, and he would not abandon them.

His ship's top speed should have been only 14.5 knots (about 16.5 miles or 27 kilometers per hour), but he turned off the steam-powered heat on the ship. This allowed his engineers to divert the extra steam to the engines, pushing *Carpathia*'s speed to over 17 knots and cutting an hour off their travel time. Rostrun posted extra lookouts to watch for icebergs and raced through the night.

By the time he arrived, the people on the lifeboats were beginning to freeze to death. If he had taken an extra hour, many more would have died. His ship took on all 705 survivors—more than it was designed to hold—but there was nothing they could do for the 1,500 people who had already drowned or frozen.

Survivors of the Titanic *disaster on board the* Carpathia. *Image courtesy of the Library of Congress.*

So, what happened to the ship the *Titanic* crew and passengers had seen earlier? Which captain and crew sat by or sailed on while over a thousand people died in those arctic waters? While the *Titanic* disaster is a tragedy and a warning about the dangers of overconfidence, it's also a mystery. That other ship might have saved many lives, and no one knows who it was or where it went.

The *Californian* took the blame at the time. The cargo ship was certainly closer than the *Carpathia* and could have reached the *Titanic* sooner. Why didn't it come to the rescue? Was it the ship that the dying *Titanic* passengers watched with hope turning to despair?

To understand the debate over the *Californian,* it's helpful to compare its timeline with the *Titanic*'s that night. Keep in mind that clocks on ships could be several minutes off from each other depending on how and when the time was set. Like the *Titanic* and the *Carpathia,* the *Californian* was traveling from the United Kingdom to the United States. The night the *Titanic* sank, the *Californian* encountered icebergs in the area and broadcasted a warning to other ships nearby, including the *Titanic.* That section of the Atlantic Ocean was like a highway for the many ships traveling between Europe and North America, so other ships were always within radio distance. By 10:00 that night, the *Californian* stopped, afraid of hitting an iceberg in the dark. The *Titanic* sailed on, confident in its "unsinkable" design.

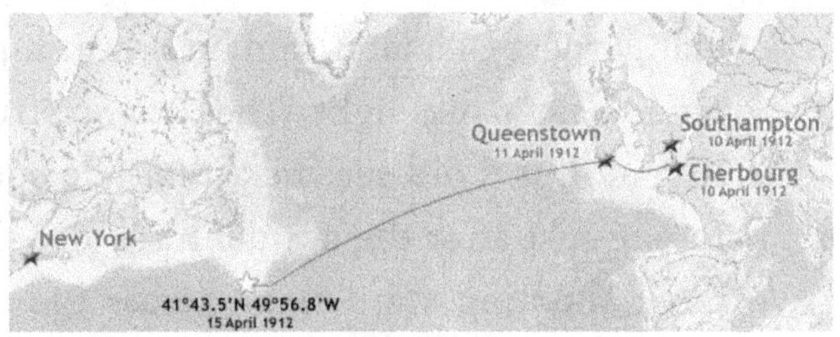

A map showing the Titanic's path from Ireland toward the United States and where it sank. Many ships traveled this route, so it was reasonable to believe that another vessel would be close. Image courtesy of prioryman via Wikimedia under a GNU license.

The *Californian*'s crew sat in the stillness and watched shooting stars streak across the velvet blackness of the night. The radio operator went to bed for the night. He forgot to set the alert system that would have warned him if emergency messages came through, like those the *Titanic* would soon be sending.

Before falling asleep, the *Californian*'s captain, Captain Lord, noticed lights in the distance. He guessed it to be another ship about five miles away. He and a crew member discussed the lights.

"It's the *Titanic*," the crewman suggested.

"No," the captain said. "It can't be. It's too small."

After all, the *Titanic* was a floating city at 52,000 tons. The *Californian* and most other ships of the time were a fraction of the size, under 10,000 tons.

Finally, after watching the mystery lights for a while, Captain Lord retired for the night.

But the *Californian* wasn't entirely asleep. The night watchman also noted the lights of the other ship and, like the captain, guessed the vessel to be five miles away.

One crewman, Ernest Gill, later said he saw a ship about ten miles away at nearly midnight. The *Titanic* struck the iceberg at 11:40 p.m. If Gill did see the *Titanic*, he spotted it either just before or just after the accident. He also thought he saw two more shooting stars blaze across the sky but wondered if they might be flares from another ship. Flares weren't always a sign of distress—they could be used to send other signals—so he decided it wasn't his concern and went to bed at about 12:30 a.m. At that time, the *Titanic* began lowering its lifeboats.

Second Officer Stone of the *Californian*, on duty for the night watch, spotted several flares starting at about 12:45 a.m. It wasn't until an hour later at 1:45 a.m. that he finally decided to wake the captain about them. At that point, the *Titanic* was still above water, but it was tipping dangerously as the sea filled its belly. Captain Lord, woken from sleep, suggested that his second officer send a Morse code message with flashing lights to the other ship to see if they were in trouble. Stone sent the Morse code message, but the other ship did not reply.

On the *Titanic* at that time, passengers and crew realized the ship was sinking faster. Second Officer Lightoller, Stone's counterpart on the *Titanic*, was launching the lifeboats, along with First Officer Murdoch. The *Titanic* was tilted forward so far that the lifeboats were only 10 feet from the water, instead of 75 feet as normal. Lightoller and Murdoch did not fully load each lifeboat; they were rushing to get the boats into the water. Some passengers still thought they had a better chance by staying with the *Titanic* until rescue came, and no one was sure if the lifeboats could really hold their full load while lowered from the ship. After all, the lifeboats were only meant to move passengers to a waiting rescue ship. Lightoller expected the boat he saw in the distance to take on the survivors and then perhaps send the lifeboats back for more. The *Titanic* sent its own Morse code light signals to the neighboring ship, but it did not respond.

At about 2:00 a.m., Officer Stone on the *Californian* said the other ship's lights vanished as it sailed away.

At 2:10 a.m., the *Titanic*'s bow (front) tilted so far underwater that its lights flickered out. At 2:17 a.m., the

Titanic snapped in two, and a few minutes later, both halves sank.

The *Carpathia* steamed at full speed through dangerous waters to reach the survivors, while the much closer *Californian* slept for the night.

Those on the *Californian* who rose first in the morning saw another ship (probably the *Mount Royal,* which arrived after the *Carpathia* to see if they could help) and assumed it was the ship they had seen the night before. Only later that morning did they learn that the *Titanic* had sunk and rescue efforts were underway almost right under their noses. They hurried over to the *Carpathia*, about nineteen miles away, and offered to help, but it was too late: the *Carpathia* had picked up every survivor, and the *Californian* was left to sail among the bodies of the dead bobbing in their life vests, some of whom they might have saved if they had paid more attention to the signals of distress they had seen through the night.

Sea rescues are complex—lowering lifeboats, pulling people from the water who might be too stiff with cold to hold onto a rope, and hauling them up into the ship—so, even if another ship had been there before 2:00 a.m., some passengers would likely have gone into the water and frozen to death, especially because of the lack of enough lifeboats. It took the *Carpathia* about four hours to pull all the lifeboat survivors on board, and that was only 705 people of more than 2,200 passengers and crew; anyone in the water did not have that much time to wait. Another ship might have reduced the rescue time and saved lives, though.

Captain Rostrun receives an award for his service from Titanic *survivor and philanthropist Margaret Brown. Later called "The Unsinkable Molly Brown," she helped other passengers off the ship as it sank and organized funds for the poorer passengers after their rescue. Image courtesy of Bain News Service and the Library of Congress.*

Captain Lord and the *Californian* were widely condemned after the disaster for their inaction. Officer Lightoller—who went down with the *Titanic* but was able to swim to one of the lifeboats—as well as Officer Boxhall and other survivors insisted that they had seen another ship no more than five miles distant, and the *Californian* was the only ship known to be in the area. Officer Stone of the *Californian* testified that the lights he saw vanish at about 2:00 a.m. had gone slowly like a ship sailing away, but many believed he saw the *Titanic*'s lights flash out when its power cut at 2:10 a.m. And Ernest Gill's testimony that he had seen a large ship no more than ten miles away from the *Californian* condemned Captain Lord, though some people pointed out that Gill had been paid a year's salary by a newspaper for his story and questioned his honesty.

Captain Lord defended himself. It had not been the *Californian* that was so close, he insisted. He had seen a smaller ship five miles away—a the ship that had been between him and the *Titanic* and had let 1,500 people die. That ship must have seen both the *Titanic*'s and the *Californian*'s Morse code signals as well as the flares and ignored them all, sailing away as the *Titanic* went under. The *Californian* had made mistakes, especially not turning on its emergency warning system, but Captain Lord claimed it had been too far away, at almost twenty miles from the disaster with icebergs blocking the way, to see or understand what was happening.

Though much smaller than the Titanic, the Californian might have been able to save some victims from the icy water. Image courtesy of Wikimedia.

For decades, Captain Lord was widely regarded as a coward and a liar. Then, in 1985, explorers and scientists using robots deep on the ocean floor found the remnants of the *Titanic.* This is significant because the exact spot where the ship sank had long been a mystery. Was it less than ten miles from the *Californian* as Gill suggested? The *Titanic* had sent two different locations in its distress signal, and it could have drifted more after the message was sent. This meant that no one knew for sure how far the *Titanic* was from the

Californian. Lightoller and Boxhall had seen a ship close at hand, and who could it be but the *Californian*?

Who indeed. Because the *Titanic*'s wreckage was found seventeen miles from the *Californian*'s position—about as far as Captain Lord had insisted he was located from the disaster. Assuming the *Titanic* didn't drift much as it was sinking, Lord could not have seen the *Titanic,* and more to the point, the crew and passengers of the *Titanic* likely would not have seen the lights of the *Californian.* Its position certainly did not match with Officer Boxhall's description of a ship sailing *toward* the *Titanic.*

Marine historians still think Lord was negligent in not acting sooner to signs of a ship in distress, but some are now convinced that he was not within sight of the sinking ship. If the *Californian* had not been the ship that was so close to the *Titanic,* then who was?

There may have been other small ships in the area that didn't have radios, like "tramp steamers" or small steamships that took irregular shipping work. They wouldn't have heard the *Titanic*'s distress call, but they would have seen the flares and the Morse code lights and perhaps even spotted the lifeboats going out on the water. Even if they were too small to take on many survivors, they might have put extra lifeboats in the water. Why would they have ignored the *Titanic*'s disaster?

One possibility is that the other ship was doing something illegal. A crew member on the seal-hunting ship *Samson* later said that he thought he saw the *Titanic*'s flares that night, but that his ship ignored them because they were hunting illegally. People studying the *Samson*'s route doubt it was close to the *Titanic* that night. But if another ship was doing something illegal in the area, it might have bypassed the *Titanic* to avoid being caught.

There are also questions about the *Mount Temple* passenger ship and a tramp steamer that passed near the disaster site called the *Almerian.*

The *Mount Temple* said that as it was racing to the disaster site to help with the rescue, it passed a small ship leaving the area—maybe running away from the sinking after it failed to help? The *Carpathia* also mentioned passing a smaller ship. And the *Californian* insisted there was a smaller ship between itself and the *Titanic.* Their descriptions of this tramp steamer suggest it was the *Almerian* sneaking away from disaster.

But the *Almerian* claimed it never came that close to the *Titanic*'s location. It, in turn, casts doubts on the *Mount Temple*'s story that it only arrived in the area after the rescue mission had ended. The *Almerian* said it was near the ice field at 3 a.m. and passed another ship. It used Morse code lamp signals to try to identify the other ship. Because of the strange effects of the cold air that night, the *Almerian* could only make out part of the reply, the letters: O-U-N-T. The *Mount Temple*'s route should have taken it safely around the ice field, but maybe it took the more dangerous route to shave some time off its trip, against company orders, and it avoided helping the *Titanic* so it wouldn't be caught. Some historians have noted that its logbook for that night seems incomplete, and the captain's later testimony of his actions was inconsistent.

Most concerning, one of the *Mount Temple*'s passengers

later claimed to have seen the *Titanic*'s distress flares. Sometimes people pretend to have been more involved in dramatic events than they were because it makes them feel important (such as claiming to see the flares instead of only being on a rescue ship that arrived too late)—and sometimes under stress, we remember things incorrectly—so one person's story hasn't been enough to condemn the *Mount Temple* completely, but it does cast suspicion on the ship.

While the *Almerian* and *Mount Temple* pointed fingers at each other, it's possible that either or both of them were close to the *Titanic* that night and tried to hide their mistake in not going to the rescue. It's also possible that they were near each other in the ice field, but not close enough to have seen or helped the *Titanic*.

So what happened that night? Did some trick of the still darkness and smooth water allow the *Californian* and *Titanic* to see each other when they were actually many miles apart? Were the *Mount Temple* or *Almerian* closer than they let on, and they tried to hide their cowardice in not helping a ship in need? Or was some other ship in the area with a nefarious purpose that it hid by sailing past the sinking ship?

Ultimately, the *Titanic*'s passengers died because the ship wasn't prepared for a disaster. They never even held an emergency evacuation drill. The *Titanic* relied too much on the promise of progress. Future ships would be built better and have more lifeboats and radios because of the lessons learned from the disaster. But more lives might have been saved if another ship had been there sooner—or if a closer ship had heeded the call for help.

CHAPTER TWO

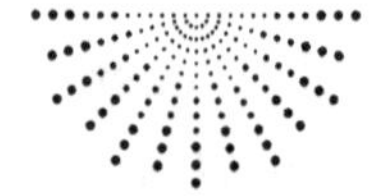

Who Killed John Parr?

John Parr's tombstone says he was twenty years old when he died in World War I, fighting the Germans in Belgium, but that's not true. In fact, he had just turned seventeen. He lied about his age to join the British Army when he was only fourteen—probably one of the youngest soldiers in the British Army. His tombstone also says he died on the 21st of August 1914. If that's true, then he was the first British soldier to die in action in World War I. The problem is, no one is certain when John Parr died—or who killed him. The truth about John Parr's death is a mystery buried in the rubble of two World Wars.

Parr was in Belgium in 1914 for the first British battle of the "Great War," as World War I was known at the time. Tensions had been brewing between the nations of Europe for years, and their leaders had formed a web of alliances. Germany was allied with Austria-Hungary, Bulgaria, and the Ottoman Empire. France's allies included the United Kingdom and Russia. This meant that if one country started a war, it would create a domino effect, dragging all of Europe and their overseas colonies into the bloodshed. When a Serbian rebel assassinated an Austrian archduke in June of 1914, it was the match that lit the dynamite. Europe exploded.

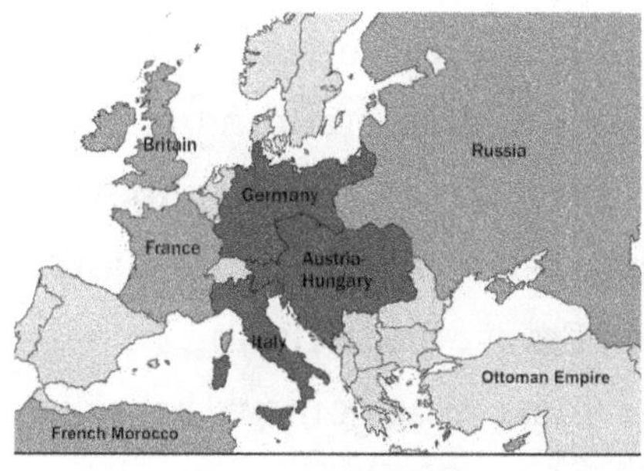

Germany, Austria-Hungary, and Italy were allied at first against Britain, France, and Russia, though Italy later changed sides. The Ottoman Empire, just below Russia, eventually allied itself with Germany and Austria-Hungary, while the United States and Japan joined on the side of Britain, France, and Russia. With colonies around the globe, these alliances dragged the whole world into war. Image courtesy of Nydas via Wikimedia.

Each nation had been developing new weapons and strategies and believed that their technologies were the best. Many rulers and leaders trusted they would quickly win the war, prove their superiority, and expand their power and resources in this "Great War."

Kaiser Wilhelm II, the ruler of Germany, told his troops,

"You will be home before the leaves have fallen from the trees."

He was terribly and fatally wrong.

Germany had long planned how they would attack France, whose lands they hoped to carve away. They would march across the north and take Paris, crushing the heart of France and forcing a surrender. And France would never expect it. Why?

Because of Belgium. Belgium was a small country that had been hammered by so many wars between its bigger neighbors that they finally came to an arrangement. Belgium agreed not to have a large standing army or engage in any wars. In exchange, all of its neighbors signed a treaty agreeing to leave Belgium alone. Germany had signed that treaty along with France and Britain.

And now, Germany was going to break it.

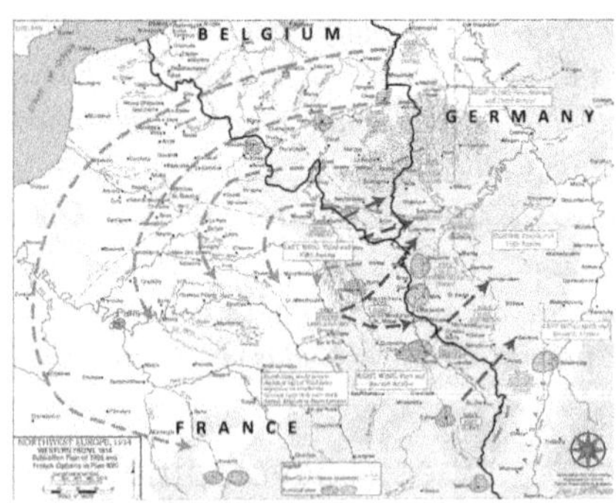

Germany's Schlieffen Plan involved swinging north through Belgium to strike Paris and the back of France's armies, who Germany assumed would avoid Belgium according to their treaty. Image courtesy of the US Military.

As far as Germany was concerned, it was only planning

to break the treaty a little. It wasn't attacking Belgium or asking it to fight. It only wanted Belgium to stand aside and turn a blind eye while Germany marched through Belgium to get to France. Certainly, Germany said when it sent its demands to Belgium's king, that wasn't too much to ask of a good neighbor. Germany promised to leave Belgium alone. As long as Belgium did exactly as Germany asked.

The Belgian king, Albert I, was horrified by Germany's demands. He was faced with a terrible decision: Either he broke Belgium's treaty and subjected his people to occupation by German forces, or he asked his people to fight to defend their nation's integrity.

King Alfred knew what he had to do.

He responded, "Belgium is a nation, not a road."

He called for help from the other signers of the treaty and summoned the small national guard to the city of Liege near the Belgian-German border to hold out as long as possible so that Britain and France could come to their aid. Belgium could not win—not against the number of soldiers that Germany had piled on their borders—but they could delay long enough for help to come.

They made the Germans fight for every inch of Belgian soil. The Germans, offended that Belgium had not accepted their offer, treated the Belgians as traitors. They killed men, women, and children, and burned entire cities, destroying ancient churches and libraries full of priceless, irreplaceable medieval books. Belgium's resistance made them heroes around the world.

And it gave time for Britain's army, including John Parr's 4th Battalion, to arrive.

The ruins of the library at Louvain, Belgium, filled with the remains of ancient books burned by the Germans in 1914. Image courtesy of The New York Times *via the Internet Archive.*

Britain's newspapers declared, "Germany tried to bribe us with peace to desert our friends and duty. But Great Britain has preferred the path of honour."

John Parr arrived in Belgium with the British forces in August. The BBC reported that Parr's superior officers described him as "clean, sober and intelligent... inclined to be insubordinate." The teenager from a working class family had joined the army perhaps looking for regular meals and a touch of adventure, but now his country was at war, and his company stood in the shadow of the German army.

The Germans planned to be halfway to Paris by that time, but almost three weeks into the war, they hadn't made it past the little medieval city of Mons on the Belgium border with France. The British army was much larger than the Belgian one, but still smaller than the German forces.

Parr's battalion prepared to face the enemy at Mons, a Belgian city near the French border.

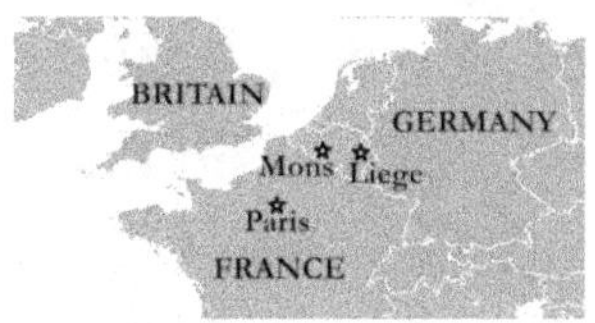

The German armies had hoped to be in Paris before Britain could join the war, but it still hadn't made it out of Belgium, having fought from Liege to Mons.

This is where Parr's trail turns fuzzy. World War I was an odd mixture of modern and historical: horseback charges against machine guns, bicycles riding between landmines, swords giving way to flamethrowers. And the records were just as disjointed. We don't even have a photograph of John Parr—like many young men of his time, he never had one taken. Now, we're used to having records of everything. Between social media and digital records of many moments of our lives, most of us leave a trail through the world.

Soldiers from Britain's colony in India mounted on horseback and armed with spears. Most soldiers went into World War I unprepared for the new technologies they would face. Image courtesy of the German Federal Archive and Wikimedia.

Yet the world was different then, and John Parr disappeared. His mother Alice didn't hear from him for months and wrote to the British War Office in 1915 to see where he was. The War Office said that he was still with his military unit. But, when they checked on him, they discovered he was not with his battalion.

The BBC report quoted from Alice Parr's concerned letters. "I've not heard from him at all and the War Office can tell me nothing... I have heard from Berlin. The address is from a prisoner of war—one of my son's chums—to say that my son was shot down at Mons."

The War Office dug into the mystery. We don't know exactly what they found, because their records were destroyed in 1940 when the Nazis bombed London during World War II. We do know they didn't come up with an exact answer about John Parr's death, but they decided that he had, indeed, died somewhere around the time of the Battle of Mons. They placed the headstone for him declaring his death to be August 21st—two days before the battle. Whatever evidence they used to choose that day is now lost.

We're left with rumors and guesses about what happened to John Parr in Mons.

One soldier who worked as a bicycle scout later said that Parr was also sent on a bicycle to spy out the German positions on the night of August 21st. The other scout was surprised to see the death date on Parr's headstone, but he recalled that he saw Parr that night and then never again. Existing records don't show that Parr worked as a scout, or even that scouts went out on August 21st, though several orderlies were sent in the early hours of August 22nd to gather the troops in preparation for battle. Maybe the other soldier remembered some facts wrong, or maybe some of the records were lost.

Bicycles were common transportation in World War I. These bicycle scouts are walking their bikes through the mud past a ruined town. Image courtesy of National Library of Scotland and Wikimedia.

A story collected many years after the war from an elderly Belgian woman may tell us Parr's fate. The woman was only eight at the Battle of Mons. She remembers seeing two British bicycle scouts that night, two days before the battle would start. The British scouts came across a German soldier or scout.

"Go back to base and warn them," the first scout said, waving his companion back.

This first scout held his ground against the German, holding him off with his gun, while the second scout pedaled back to warn the others.

The Belgian woman recalled the German dashing through her garden to shoot the first scout, leaving him to die in the ditch beside the road. She believed the dead bicycle scout was John Parr.

This could be the fate of John Parr, but some people have questioned it. For one thing, it relies on a woman remembering an event from many decades earlier and identifying the dead British scout as John Parr without even a photograph to be certain who he was.

There is also no mention of this incident in existing British or German military records. If the second British scout returned and reported what he saw, someone should have made a note of it, and of the missing scout. Yet, it is possible that the second scout didn't make it back either, and that the German likewise died before he had a chance to report his encounter.

Military historians doubt that the Germans were that close to the British on August 21st, though. They say John Parr shouldn't have encountered any Germans that night. But the German could have been a scout. Or, maybe he was trying to desert—run away from the fighting—and so never told anyone.

John may have tried to desert as well, with battle looming, though we have no reason to suspect that he did. It's only one of many things that might have happened in the dark night of August 21, 1914.

Another possibility is that John was killed by friendly fire, when someone accidentally kills one of their allies. The Belgians had been under attack by German soldiers who would destroy their homes and murder their families, so they may have been quick to shoot at anyone in a military uniform. Or, another British or even French scout may have mistaken Parr for one of the enemies and shot him. If this was the case, the person who shot him may have realized their mistake too late and hidden it, making John disappear.

We only know that the last anyone claims they saw John Parr was on August 21st.

It's possible that John made it back and joined his unit for the Battle of Mons. No one specifically remembered seeing him there, but no one remembered missing him, either. All but 32 of the men in Parr's Company D were captured or killed. The survivors later recounted the men they saw die at Mons, and John Parr wasn't one of them, but 1,600 British soldiers died in the fight, and Parr could have been lost in the confusion of battle.

Fighting on the Western Front along the borders of Germany, Belgium, and France turned into trench warfare. Both sides fought from deep trenches that were often full of rats and mud. Sometimes the dead were lost and buried in the mud of the trenches. Image courtesy of Imperial War Museums and Wikimedia.

In the Voices of the First World War project, stretcher bearer William Collins described the chaos of Mons: "In that wood, to the entrance to that wood I heard the first shell burst above my head—it was a shrapnel shell—with a highish burst, white smoke and the bullets came down whistling like all the hobs of hell, as if 1000 whistles had been turned on."

The British stood their ground through brutal fighting, but eventually the German's massive number of troops forced the British to fall back, leaving their injured and dead to be captured by the Germans or buried in mass graves. Was John among the fallen, one of many who would die too young and rest with thousands of others under Belgian soil? Or maybe he died later in a German prisoner of war camp, his name somehow lost to history.

Regardless of which story of John's death is accurate, he was likely one of the first British soldiers to die in action—one of the first of 880,000 British victims of the war, and of 9 million soldiers of all nationalities who died over the four years. The war also left 10 million civilians dead, 20 million people injured, and countless more with their houses burned to ash and rubble. The stand-off between new technologies made the fighting grind to a halt, and the armies dug lines of trenches that cut down the face of Europe like a bleeding gash where 6,000 soldiers died every day. Villages were bombed off the maps, and entire forests were shattered to splinters of wood and gaping holes in the ground. Poison gasses and brutal new weapons took their toll on the whole generation. No longer did most people look to technology with hope, but instead feared the future and mourned the dead.

The headstone for John Parr commemorates him in a military cemetery in Belgium, though no body is buried there. The date on it, 21 August 1914, reflects the last time anyone is certain they saw him alive. Perhaps he was the first Briton to die in WWI, though we may never know for certain. Quite by accident, his marker sits directly across from George Edwin Ellison. Ellison was the last British soldier to die in action in World War I, killed by a sniper, also in Mons, Belgium, just an hour and a half before the war ended on November 11, 1918.

John Parr's tombstone in Belgium. No body is buried here since he was never found. Image courtesy of Wernervc license CC-BY-SA 4.0.

CHAPTER THREE

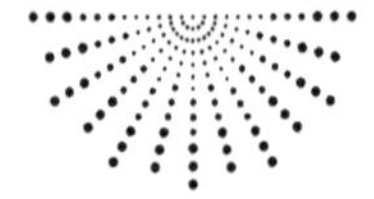

The Tsar's Lost Treasures

Modern Americans from John D. Rockefeller to Bill Gates are famous for becoming billionaires with their technological innovations and keen business sense. None of them, however, have become as rich as Tsar Nicholas II of Russia. When World War I started, he was one of the wealthiest people who had ever lived. By the end of the war, he and his family were dead, his government was overthrown, and his vast wealth was scattered—with some of it still missing today. For the last hundred years, people have been hunting for the tsar's lost riches. Occasionally, they even find a missing treasure, so there may be more riches and more history left to discover.

In 1914, Tsar Nicholas's Russia was a massive empire

with 150 million people and one of the largest gold supplies in the world. Russia entered World War I as an ally of France and Britain fighting against Germany. This forced Germany to fight on two fronts: the Western Front against the French and British forces, and the Eastern Front against Russia. While the Western Front remained so evenly matched that soldiers on both sides dug trenches and defended battle lines that changed little after the first year of war, Russia continually lost ground and lost soldiers to the Germans. Russians were suffering and dying, and Nicholas and his Romanov family didn't seem to take the problem seriously.

Tsar Nicholas with the Tsarina Alexandra and their four daughters and son. They lived in luxury removed from the problems of ordinary Russians. Image courtesy of the Library of Congress and Wikimedia.

Nicholas had inherited his power and wealth and hadn't been trained or prepared to manage it.

When his father died, he said, "What is going to happen to me and all of Russia? I am not prepared to be a Tsar. I never wanted to become one. I know nothing of the business of ruling." He clung to outdated traditions, stating, "I will preserve the principle of Autocracy as firmly and unflinchingly as my late father."

Autocracy, or the rule of a single person who holds all the power, did not serve Russia well. Nicholas's unpopular, German-born wife Tsarina Alexandra, along with her favorite advisor, the self-styled prophet and mystic Grigori Rasputin, were the powers behind the throne. The Romanovs lived a lavish life of parties, fine foods, and jewels, while many of their people were starving and had very limited freedoms. Because Russia did not embrace new technologies, they were far behind other countries. Many of Russia's millions of soldiers went to war without even a gun or bullets, given instructions to take them from dead soldiers when they got the chance.

In 1917, angry Russian workers went on strike, demanding food. When soldiers were ordered to break up the strike, they instead joined the strikers in protest.

Bolsheviks (Russian communists) marching through the streets of Moscow. Image courtesy of the National Archives and Records Administration and Wikimedia.

A government official warned Nicholas, "Serious situation in the capital, where anarchy reigns. General discontent was increasing. In the streets, uninterrupted firing, and one part of the troops is firing on the other."

The Tsarina was said to reply, "This is a hooligan movement, young people run and shout that there is no bread, simply to create excitement, along with workers who prevent others from working. If the weather were very cold they would probably all stay at home."

The Tsar didn't respond to the problem, and the protests increased.

The end of the Romanovs' time had come.

Germany, seeing an opportunity to end the war on the Eastern Front and devote its attention to the Western Front, snuck exiled Russian communist leader Vladimir Lenin back into Russia. He led the Bolshevik Revolution in overthrowing the old regime and establishing the communist government of the Soviet Union that would rule Russia for much of the twentieth century.

One of the ideas behind communism was to take wealth from the rich and distribute it to the common people. People, however, seem to have a hard time sharing. That was certainly the case with the vast riches of the Romanov family. Much of the Romanovs' riches went missing and may still be out there, waiting to be "redistributed" to whomever is lucky enough to find it.

The largest single chunk of missing wealth was the vast gold supplies of the Russian Government. Before the outbreak of war, Nicholas had 500 tons of gold (worth billions of dollars), which he sent to the city of Kazan to keep it farther from the German armies. Once the Revolution began, the Bolshevik army attacked Kazan. Forces loyal to the Romanovs snuck the gold out of the city on a train going east to save it from the revolutionaries. The revolutionaries gave chase on another train—though, trains being slower then than now, the chase actually took many weeks.

The gold-filled train finally came to the city of Irkutsk near Lake Baikal, the deepest freshwater lake in the world. There, the slow train chase came to an end. A group of Czeck soldiers who had been hired to fight for Russia in the Great War were stranded there by the Revolution. They seized the gold, trading it to the Bolsheviks for the chance to leave Russia and go home.

But it appears that the Bolsheviks didn't get all the gold: they were short by about 200 tons. That much gold would add you to the list of billionaires with John D. Rockefeller and Bill Gates. So, this was not just a case of a few soldiers sticking a little gold in their pockets. What happened to all that money?

A single bar of gold like this is worth almost $90,000 in 2024 US money. Imagine a trainload of them. Image by scanrail via Deposit Photos.

Local rumors said that either the Russians loyal to the Romanovs or the Czech soldiers buried the gold in the nearby woods, planning to come back for it later. If that's true, there's a huge fortune in Siberia waiting to be found.

Others say the gold went east with the Czech soldiers on a train that crashed and fell into the depths of Lake Baikal. This lake is so huge that it's a mile deep and contains one-fifth of all the surface fresh water in the world. This makes it difficult to explore, but scientists are beginning to discover what's at the bottom of the lake. Recent diving expeditions have uncovered the wreckage of a train in those dark, cold waters. The robot divers also picked up shiny spots on their cameras. Could this be some of the tsar's lost gold? We don't know, because the robots weren't able to gather any of the shiny substance from among the rocks and other debris at the bottom of the lake.

While the tsar's gold went east, the revolutionaries put the tsar, tsarina, and the five Romanov children under house arrest in the country. They were allowed to take some of their personal possessions with them—including their jewelry. The story goes that the Romanovs befriended the monks and nuns near where they were imprisoned, and that the monks helped them hide their jewels in the hopes that they could come back for them or perhaps use the money to start a new life elsewhere.

Unfortunately, the Tsar's family would never escape Russia. The revolutionaries secretly executed the entire family. For many years, people believed that Nicholas's daughter Anastasia survived the massacre. In fact, when a historian found the hidden grave of the Romanovs, two of the children's bodies were absent. But in 2007, the two missing children were found buried not far from the rest of their family. DNA testing confirmed their relationship. Sadly, all of the Romanov children were dead. Many people believe the jewels they had hoped to come back for are still buried somewhere in the area.

One Russian treasure we know is still missing are the Romanov Faberge Easter Eggs. Faberge is a company renowned for its beautiful goldwork. Starting in 1885 and continuing through 1917, the tsar gave his wife an Easter egg each year—but not just any Easter egg. These elaborate "eggs" were made of gold and jewels and often opened up to show a treasure inside like more jewels or tiny clocks. A few other wealthy Russian aristocrats copied the tsar's idea, so that about 70 Faberge Eggs were made in total, of which 50 were Imperial or Romanov Faberge Eggs. The Revolutionaries seized most of the eggs, claiming them for the state, but only 42 of them were accounted for. The other eight were missing—perhaps sold or smuggled out of the country.

The Lily of the Valley Faberge Egg. Image courtesy of Pedro Szekely license CC-BY-SA 2.0

In 2014, a man found a gold-colored egg at an antique

store in the Midwestern United States. He thought he would melt it down for the metals, but he decided first to find out more about it. It turned out to be one of the eight missing Imperial Eggs, and he sold it for $33 million. So, there's hope that the other seven eggs might turn up, assuming they were never melted down for their gold and jewels. In fact, in 2022, a wealthy Russian's yacht was seized as part of punishments against Russian leaders for attacking neighboring Ukraine. The yacht was full of valuable artwork—including what might be another of the missing eggs. Experts have yet to reveal if the egg is real, but if it is, there are still six eggs left to find—the most valuable Easter egg hunt in history!

CHAPTER FOUR

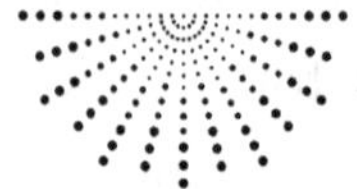

Deadly Beauty Sleep

In 1926, the "Roaring Twenties" were in full swing. Young people, weary from World War I and the Influenza Pandemic that swept the globe from 1918 to 1920, wanted to throw off the past and have a good time. It was a thrilling era for many women who were gaining the right to vote and other freedoms. Many embraced their new freedom as "flappers" who cut their hair short and enjoyed new dance styles like the Charleston. Rose R. of New York City was one of those young people. She loved to go to parties and paint and even learned to fly an airplane. Life was exciting.

Then, one night, Rose had a dream that she was trapped in a castle. In the dream, she fell under an enchantment that transformed her into a living statue. As night turned into morning, she was still exhausted—so exhausted that her family struggled to wake her up. When she did wake, she couldn't speak and could barely move. Her nightmare had come true. Rose had become the latest—and one of the last—victims of a mysterious disease called Sleepy Sickness.

Rose went from having fun like these flappers dancing the Charleston to not being able to wake up or move. Photo courtesy of National Photo Co and the Library of Congress.

Sleepy Sickness showed up in Europe in 1916 while most of the globe was distracted by the World War. According to Sleepy Sickness expert Dr. Oliver Sacks, it would go on to kill or disable at least five million people. Even today, no one knows where it came from, what caused it, why it suddenly disappeared—or if it might ever return.

The first report of the case probably came from a doctor in Vienna, Austria who noted several patients with strange symptoms. Some had delirium, seeing things that weren't there or talking nonsense. A few showed swelling in their brains. But the symptom that stumped him was their exhaustion. It wasn't that they were tired of the war or in need of a nap or a vacation: they could not stay awake, no matter how much sleep they got. Their symptoms didn't fit any disease he knew.

At about the same time, a battlefield doctor in France noticed similar symptoms in some of the soldiers under his care. Delirium. Aches and trembling. And exhaustion so deep they would fall asleep in the middle of a conversation.

By 1918, doctors in England were sharing stories about what they thought was an outbreak of the Botulism bacteria often found in spoiled food. People ranging in age from 9 to 70 developed exhaustion, headaches, trembling, slurred speech, weakness that kept them in bed, and sometimes even paralysis. The patients were spread around the country. None of them lived in the same house, ate the same foods, or had anything obvious in common. The doctors ran all the tests they knew and could not find any cause for the sickness.

Under the shadow of the war, this new disease spread, probably starting somewhere in Eastern Europe and eventually reaching North America and as far as Central America and India. Because doctors in different countries weren't sharing information during the war, they didn't realize at first they were dealing with a new disease or how far it was spreading.

This is not African Sleeping Sickness, which is caused by a parasite. European Sleeping or “Sleepy” Sickness, called

Encephalitis lethargica ("swelling of the brain and exhaustion") by scientists, often started with symptoms similar to influenza: aches, fever, sore throat, upset stomach. But then it became something much different. Victims might become confused or delirious, see or hear hallucinations, or experience the severe burning of nerve pain like electricity shooting through their limbs. Sometimes they developed sudden tremors or paralysis.

And they slept. They could fall asleep in the middle of eating. In New York City, people dropped into slumber on the subway trains and had to be hauled off to the hospital. A young man in Britain reached out to catch a ball in a game of cricket (similar to American baseball), and he froze in that position. They carried him off the field with the ball still caught in his hand.

Some fell asleep and never woke.

About a third of those who developed Sleepy Sickness slipped into a deep stupor, and no amount of shouting, shaking, or medical treatments could awaken them. These eventually died.

In a variation of the disease, instead of being unable to wake, patients were unable to sleep. They couldn't stop moving, talking, or thinking, and if they didn't recover and rest in time, they died of exhaustion.

For those who survived, their ordeal wasn't necessarily over.

The Health Ministry in London was quoted in The Indianapolis Times saying, "We don't know what causes sleeping sickness in Europe, and we don't know as yet what precautions are necessary to prevent its spread... One of the most terrible aspects of the disease is that even if the victim recovers, he is almost invariably left with some grave physical or mental defect. Sometimes, too, it makes a fundamental change in the victim's character. Cases are on record where a person of unquestionable truthfulness emerged from the sickness as a colossal liar."

Sometimes within days, and sometimes years later, the survivors faced the next phase of Sleepy Sickness. This involved various symptoms much like another illness that's difficult to trace or treat called Parkinson's Disease. Patients might tremble uncontrollably or have their muscles go absolutely rigid so they can't move. Many remained in a half-awake state like they were sleepwalking, not really interacting with the world around them.

A few patients could escape their "locked" state if something triggered them to move. For one woman, it was music. One man would only "wake" if someone tossed him a ball or something else to kick around. A woman sat unmoving in a wheelchair until someone threw her a set of oranges, which she would juggle. If she dropped one, she would instantly "turn off" again.

The young man who froze in the middle of the cricket game survived but sometimes in later life he would lock up and reach his arm out exactly as he had when Sleepy Sickness seized him. He had no control over this. It was like something in him was trapped in that moment in 1919.

Rose R., the "sleeping beauty" with the nightmare of being trapped in a castle, stayed in a dreamlike state until 1969 when Dr. Oliver Sacks tried an experimental Parkinson's drug on the Sleepy Sickness patients in his hospital. The drug helped these patients "wake up." They could move and speak again after so many years of being frozen. Rose said that she was aware of what was happening in the world, such as World War II, but all of that felt like a dream to her, and to her, she still lived in 1926. In fact, like many of the Sleepy Sickness patients, she looked much younger than her actual years, almost like she was frozen in time.

Dr. Oliver Sacks was noted for his understanding of Sleepy Sickness and for his compassion dealing with its survivors. Image courtesy of the Library of Congress.

Unfortunately, the positive effects of Dr. Sacks' medication didn't last, and the patients, including Rose, slipped back into their sleepwalking lives. Rose still occasionally spoke, but most of the time, she was trapped once again in her nightmare castle. Without understanding the disease, there was nothing more Dr. Sacks or anyone else could do for her.

Millions of people caught Sleepy Sickness, and probably

many more sufferers went unnoticed during the war years. Most of those sickened were between the ages of 10 and 45, and the greatest number were in their teens and twenties. We don't know if this was because this age group was most susceptible to the disease, or if they were the ones most likely to be in crowded places, such as fighting in the war or working in cities.

That raises the question of how Sleepy Sickness spread. No one knows. In some cases, it seemed extremely contagious, with many people in the same building becoming sick and dying. In other cases, only a single family member became ill. It didn't seem to matter how wealthy or how clean a person was—anyone could catch Sleepy Sickness.

We likewise don't know what actually caused Sleepy Sickness. A parasite? A bacteria? A virus? Doctors at the time considered all of the possibilities but couldn't prove any of them. Some people suggested it was a toxin poisoning victims, but what toxin would suddenly be found at nearly the same time in Austria, India, England, the Philippines, South Africa—in fact, throughout the world?

The pandemic most associated with World War I is the "Spanish Flu." This influenza was called Spanish because Spain—which stayed neutral in the war and didn't need to lie to maintain morale—was one of the few countries that was honest in reporting how deadly the disease was. In all, the influenza outbreak killed at least 50 million people all over the world—and many historians believe the number is closer to 100 million. Most governments didn't admit how serious it was to prevent people panicking and hurting the war effort, even as cities like Philadelphia, Pennsylvania dug mass graves for influenza victims. Influenza killed one in every twenty or thirty people on Earth at the time and wiped out some small villages. It's remembered as one of the most deadly disease outbreaks in history.

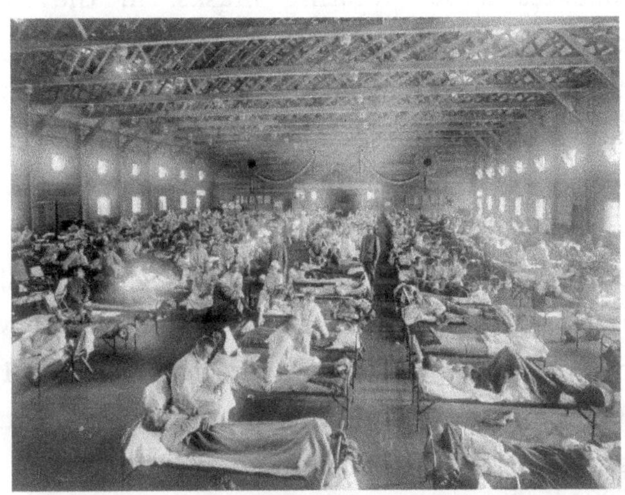

So many soldiers became ill from influenza that doctors had to build emergency hospitals like this one in Kansas to treat all the patients. Image courtesy of the National Museum of Health and Medicine.

Scientists at the time and now point to the similar timing of Spanish Flu and Sleepy Sickness. Like Sleepy Sickness, the exact origin of Spanish Flu is a mystery, but the first suspected cases of Spanish Flu were reported in Kansas, in the United States, at the beginning of 1918. Influenza had been around for a long time, but sometimes it mutates to become more deadly. That seems to be the case with Spanish Flu. US troops were gathered in training camps, preparing to join the fight in Europe. The Spanish Flu ravaged the close quarters of the US training camps, and then the troops brought the disease with them when they went overseas.

Similar to what many readers will remember from COVID-19, in 1918, schools, theaters, stores, and churches shut down during the influenza outbreak, and there were angry debates about wearing masks. In the influenza pandemic, entire families died, leaving no one to bury them. Cities created mass graves to dispose of the dead piling up in homes and morgues. Nurses, already in short supply because of the war, were in danger of being kidnapped to help care for the sick.

Doctor Franklin Martin described his own influenza symptoms, quoted in *Smithsonian Magazine*, "I was so feverish I was afraid I would ignite the clothing. I had a cough that tore my very innards out when I could not suppress it. It was dark; I surely had pneumonia and I never was so forlorn and uncomfortable in my life...When the light did finally come I was some specimen of misery—couldn't breathe without an excruciating cough and there was no hope in me."

And then the influenza mutated again, and the death rates dropped. Most of the deaths occurred in 1918 and 1919, though isolated pockets of influenza still killed for several years after. Influenza did have lingering effects on those who survived it, sometimes including severe depression and other neurological problems.

In contrast, the first suspected cases of Sleepy Sickness occurred in Eastern Europe around 1916, and the disease continued through the 1920s, disappearing by 1930.

Doctors compared the brains of those who died of Sleepy

Sickness and influenza, trying to determine if they could find a connection, but they weren't able to establish anything for certain—the brains showed very different types of damage from the two illnesses. Yet the H1N1 influenza outbreak of 2009 was followed by an increase in narcolepsy, which is trouble staying awake, or feeling tired all the time (though it doesn't have all of the other symptoms of Sleepy Sickness). So, scientists still wonder if there might be a connection.

One theory is that the two diseases from different continents collided to form a "perfect storm" of deadly illness. It could be that infection with Spanish Flu made people more susceptible to the bacteria or virus that causes Sleepy Sickness. People might have survived one sickness too weak to fight the other.

Other doctors suggested that Sleepy Sickness might have been an auto-immune disease: an illness where the body attacks itself, sometimes after some kind of triggering event—for instance, an infection with influenza. But Sleepy Sickness started before the influenza outbreak (as far as we know), and not everyone who developed Sleepy Sickness had been sick with influenza. If Sleepy Sickness is an auto-immune disease, its appearance and disappearance remain just as mysterious as before.

Studying the brains of those who died of Sleepy Sickness did show signs of serious infection in the brain. The part of the brain most infected might have influenced which symptoms the person had and how sick they got. Like we have seen with COVID-19, people's immune systems react differently to new diseases—what is deadly to some can feel like a minor illness to others. In fact, some people who developed the second phase of Sleepy Sickness never knew they had the first stage of the disease.

Despite all we don't know about Sleepy Sickness, Dr. Oliver Sacks' experimental treatment offers hope that modern medicine might offer a treatment for Sleepy Sickness.

That learning and hope is important because, without knowing what caused Sleepy Sickness, we also don't know if it could happen again. There are a few records of illnesses in history that sound similar to Sleepy Sickness. And there have been rare cases since 1930 that appear to be the same illness. We can hope that such occurrences remain extremely rare or disappear altogether. But as amazing as modern medicine can be, there are still many things we don't understand about human bodies and minds, and we live in an interconnected world where an illness in one place can quickly spread across the globe. That's why historians, doctors, and scientists are always trying to learn from the past to be ready for the future.

CHAPTER FIVE

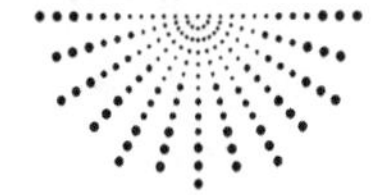

The Mummy's Curse

On April 5, 1923, a dog in England named Susie let out a heart-rending howl. According to family stories, she died just a few hours later. No one in England knew it at the time, but the dog's owner, George Herbert, Lord Carnarvon, had just died in Egypt. At Lord Carnarvon's death, the lights of Cairo flickered and went out, plunging the Egyptian city into darkness.

Lord Carnarvon died a famous man. Few remember him today, but he provided the money for one of the greatest archeological digs of the twentieth century: the excavation of KV62—the tomb of the pharaoh Tutankhamun, or King Tut. In November of 1922, Carnarvon had traveled to Egypt to be present when the archeology team broke the seal on King Tut's resting place. Carnarvon was one of the first to see the tomb, which had been sealed for 3,300 years. Along with the head archeologist Howard Carter, Carnarvon was also among the first to enter the tomb, gawking at the ancient jars filled with treasures and goods for Tutankhamun's afterlife, and especially at the gold everywhere—decorating the statues, the walls, and the sarcophagus. A few months later, he was the first to die of what many believed to be the pharaoh's curse.

The golden funeral mask of Tutankhamun was unlike anything the world had seen, but Carnarvon paid a high price for it. Image courtesy of Bjørn Christian Tørrissen license CC-BY-SA 3.0.

The discovery of Tutankhamun's tomb fascinated the

world even before rumors spread about the curse. Over the thousands of years since their burials in the Valley of the Kings, most pharaohs' tombs had been robbed of their riches. The remaining mummies and paintings on the walls provided some interesting historical information, but the treasures of the royal burials were long vanished. In fact, when Howard Carter began excavating in the Valley of the Kings in 1914, it was because the other archeologists who had bought the rights to do so had given up, declaring there was nothing left to find, and let Carter take over.

Carter believed they were wrong. Earlier archeologists had found artifacts mentioning a little-known pharaoh named Tutankhamun, but his tomb remained missing. Carter was certain this hidden treasure waited for him.

World War I delayed Carter's work, and when he did start excavations in the valley, he spent several years digging with nothing to show for it. He took a more scientific approach to archeology than his predecessors, carefully going through the rubble in the Valley of the Kings and documenting everything. Lord Carnarvon, who was paying a huge sum of money to fund Carter's work—including employing the team of Egyptian men who did most of the digging—complained that Carter was moving too slowly. So, Carter directed his team to dig beneath some ancient huts associated with the burial of a later pharaoh.

The workers grew quiet when they found a series of steps beneath the ancient huts. The Egyptian foreman, Ahmed Gerigar, notified Carter, then continued the digging until they came to a door sealed with an image of the ancient

Egyptian god Anubis. The workers stopped and stared in wonder.

They had found King Tut's tomb.

Carter sent an excited telegram to Carnarvon, "At last we have made wonderful discovery in Valley; a magnificent tomb with seals intact; re-covered same for your arrival; congratulations"

Carnarvon rushed to Egypt by steamship.

Once Carnarvon made the long horseback journey to the remote valley, Carter broke through the outer door of the tomb. Some damage in the empty first chamber suggested that someone else had broken into the tomb in ancient times, but the thief didn't go any further. Either they didn't think Tut was significant enough to rob, or something scared them away.

Carter next broke through the inner door. He prodded inside with a long pole and held a candle to check for poisonous—or flammable—gases. Then, he spent a long time peering silently into the darkness with his flashlight. The candle flickered as warm air not breathed for thousands of years escaped the tomb.

Carnarvon lost his patience. "Can you see anything?"

"Wonderful things!" Carter said.

A photograph taken by Carter's team showing one of the ancient seals they broke. Image courtesy of Wikimedia.

The tomb contained everything from ancient food stored in jars to golden jewelry to King Tut's childhood toys. Never had such an intact Egyptian royal burial been discovered.

Some of the many ancient treasures found in King Tut's tomb. Image by Harry Burton via Wikimedia.

Carter and Carnarvon invited English reporters for the grand reveal of the tomb a few days later.

While much of world marveled at the finds, many people from both Egyptian and European and American cultures were horrified to see Tutankhamun's burial disturbed and put on display. They argued this was grave robbing, pure and simple, and that the dead should be left in peace. In fact, the discovery of King Tut's tomb—and the removal of some of the artifacts overseas—was one of the things that prompted Egypt to push for more independence from Europeans.

As the world admired King Tut's treasures and Carter and Carnarvon enjoyed their fame, the warnings came through letters and telegrams: Beware of angry spirits. Beware of hidden poisons in the tomb. Beware the pharaoh's curse.

Carter and Carnarvon were not about to let superstition

or accusations of grave robbing stand in their way. Besides, they found nothing to concern them. Rumors that the tomb was engraved with a warning, "Death shall come on swift wings to whoever touches the tomb of the pharaoh," were the invention of a British author, Marie Corelli, who believed in the pharaoh's curse. The story that a cobra—a symbol of the ancient kings—ate Carter's pet canary also seems to be fiction. A few tombs from the Old Kingdom—a thousand years before King Tut's time—mentioned curses in the afterlife for those who disturbed tombs, but no such warning existed in King Tut's tomb. The archeologists believed that the pharaoh's curse was an invention of Victorian-era British writers, not ancient Egyptians.

Carter continued his careful work, documenting each item, though he sometimes chose small favorites to keep for himself. It was 1924 before he finally opened the sarcophagus to reveal the mummy.

Carter and one of his assistants examining King Tut. Image courtesy of The Times *and Wikimedia.*

By then, Carnarvon was already dead.

Carnarvon's death was not sudden. He was sick for

weeks before he died, and his demise after spending so much money on the excavations in Egypt left his family deeply in debt. He'd had a mosquito bite on his face that became infected. Some people think he developed blood poisoning from this infection. His doctor declared his cause of death as pneumonia. Most people, though, agreed with author Arthur Conan Doyle, the man who created the ever-logical Sherlock Holmes. Doyle was convinced that "elementals" set to guard the tomb had killed Carnarvon.

It was the work of the pharaoh's curse.

When Carnarvon's body was shipped back to Britain for burial, many other passengers on the boat canceled their tickets, refusing to travel with the cursed corpse. Wealthy British people had long collected ancient Egyptian artifacts. The British Museum was suddenly flooded with donations of Egyptian artifacts from collectors terrified of the curse.

The press back then was not so different from the press now: anything that got someone to buy a newspaper (or click on an article) was newsworthy. So, anyone connected with the tomb who died shortly after was declared a victim of the pharaoh's curse.

American railroad millionaire George Jay Gould visited King Tut's tomb not long after Carnarvon's death. He soon developed a fever and died—also of pneumonia—in May of 1923.

Egyptian millionaire Ali Kamel Fahmy visited the tomb with his new wife in 1923. Within weeks, she shot him to death in London. Even though she was discovered with the gun in her hand, she was acquitted of all charges—mostly because she claimed it was self defense—but some also blamed the curse.

Aubrey Herbert, Carnarvon's half-brother, died of blood poisoning from a dental surgery gone wrong several months after Carnarvon's death.

Hugh Evelyn-White, who helped with the excavations, was found dead in 1924, having written in his own blood, "I have succumbed to a curse."

Also in 1924, Sir Archibald Douglas Reid was invited to x-ray the mummy of King Tut once it was finally removed from its sarcophagus. He died before he could go. As someone who worked with radiation in its early days, though, radiation poisoning is as likely a culprit in his death as a curse.

Australian Egyptologist Arthur Mace, who worked closely with Carter in the tomb, grew ill with pleurisy (inflammation of the lungs) in 1924 and had to return to Britain. His health never recovered, and he died in 1928. Some say he was poisoned at the end.

Carter sent his friend Sir Bruce Ingram a paperweight made from a mummified hand. Other than being a questionable decorating choice, this was apparently bad luck. Ingram's house burned down, and when he tried to rebuild it, the site flooded.

Carnarvon's friend Aaron Ember died in a house fire when he went back to save a book manuscript he had been working on about the Egyptian Book of the Dead.

The curse had patience and a long arm. Richard Bethell, Carter's secretary, was found smothered to death or poisoned by an unknown person in London in 1929. His elderly and ill father fell from an upper story room of his house a few months afterwards. Many thought he had jumped, driven mad by the curse. The room from which he fell was one that contained artifacts from King Tut's tomb. Then, his funeral hearse hit and killed a young boy.

Also in 1929, Carnarvon's other half-brother, Mervyn Herbert, died of pneumonia brought on by malaria.

Howard Carter finished his work documenting the burial and survived until 1939, when he died of Hodgkin's lymphoma. This is a kind of cancer that is treatable today, but not in the 1930s. By the time of his death, Carter's fame was forgotten and his fortune gone.

Though this list might inspire one to believe in curses, there were dozens of people involved in the excavation of the tomb, and hundreds who visited it when it was first opened. We don't have many records of the Egyptian workers who helped uncover the tomb, but it appears that most lived normal lives. Carnarvon's daughter Evelyn was present with her father when the tomb was opened, and being the smallest person present, she was the first to squeeze through into some of the chambers. She lived until 1980. And today, the artifacts are on display in museums, apparently with no ill effects.

Evelyn with her father Lord Carnarvon and Howard Carter in Egypt. Image courtesy of Griffith Institute Archive.

So, was there a curse, or were the deaths the result of coincidence and poor medical care in the 1920s and 30s?

Some people look to King Tut himself for clues. Scientists, doctors, and historians have studied him and his burial for 100 years. Yet for as much as we know about Tutankhamun, there is even more we don't know. He was a boy king, and his early death at about age nineteen ended the Eighteenth Dynasty of ancient Egypt. His father was likely Ankhenaten, the pharaoh who tried to change the religion of ancient Egypt and was therefore treated as an outcast. A tomb called KV55 is probably Ankhenaten's—DNA tells us the mummy found there is King Tut's father. But the man's identity was erased—literally. After his death, someone went into his tomb, smashed the face off his sarcophagus, and scratched his name off all the walls and other markers. Whoever King Tut's father was, he wasn't a popular man.

Because King Tut died early, his burial appears to have been rushed. Some of the artifacts in his tomb were unfinished when the chambers were sealed. And as amazing as his treasures were, between his hurried burial and the unpopularity of his family line, it was probably much less impressive than most pharaohs.

Some people even believe King Tut was murdered. He has a massive crack on the back of his skull, though it might have come after his death. He also died with an unhealed broken leg, which could have led to an infection or sepsis—the same thing some people think killed Lord Carnarvon. King Tut's injury may have come from an attack, a fight, or even a fall. King Tut's foot bones show signs of a disability in his leg. One image from his tomb shows him using a walking stick, and many canes were found in his tomb, though other paintings show him fighting and hunting. So, we don't know how severe his disability was, or if he was likely to have been injured in an accident or could have defended himself against an assassin.

This ancient engraving shows King Tut with his wife. King Tut is using a walking stick or cane. Image courtesy of Tiger Cub via Wikimedia.

Doctors have also found evidence of malaria—a disease spread by mosquitos—in his mummy. Some think he has a mark on his cheek in the same place that Lord Carnarvon received the mosquito bite that made him ill.

Modern medicine can't be certain what killed the young king, but many people think his death led to a curse that later killed so many visitors to his tomb.

A different "cursed" tomb might offer a more intriguing clue to the secret of the Pharaoh's Curse. In 1973, during the restoration of Wawel Cathedral in Krakow, Poland, conservationists opened the 600-year-old tomb of King

Casimir IV Jagiellon. Within a few years of the tomb's opening, ten of the twelve team members were dead, all of mysterious illnesses. Of course, this immediately brought to mind the Pharaoh's Curse. Scientists examined the cathedral and found that it was a breeding ground for mold, especially one possible culprit: a fungus called Aspergillus. Aspergillus causes lung problems and can sometimes even lead to organ damage and the production of aflatoxins, which cause cancer—especially in people who are already sick.

The archeologists working on Casimir's tomb likely died from an especially toxic strain of Aspergillus. But what about King Tut's tomb? Could Aspergillus or a similar infection have caused his curse? After all, his tomb was sealed for thousands of years, and it was filled with decayed food, which is a breeding ground for mold and bacteria.

Yet only a small portion of the people who visited the tomb became ill. The Egyptian workers did not experience high levels of death, as far as we know. Perhaps those who had spent longer in Egypt had been exposed to the mold or bacteria and had some resistance to it. Even Carter had lived in Egypt for over a decade before he began his work. And people who were sickly were unlikely to make the long journey to the Valley of the Kings, requiring travel by boat and then by horse or donkey. That meant most of the people who were exposed to any toxins in the tomb would likely have been healthy enough to fight off infections. The exceptions would be the very wealthy Europeans and Americans who traveled despite their poor health—and would have been even more weakened by the long journey by the time they reached the tomb. Such conditions may have weakened Lord Carnarvon, George Jay Gould, and Arthur Mace.

The landscape of Valley of the Kings in Egypt is hot and remote. It's not an easy place to reach. Image courtesy of Francesco Gasparetti via Flickr license CC BY 2.0.

Aspergillus does not explain the violent deaths associated with the curse—if King Tut is to blame for those deaths, angry spirits seem like the only culprits. The fungus might partially explain the curse—or maybe not at all. Mummies—not just from Egypt, but from all over the world—have been found to contain Aspergillus spores, but there's no way to prove that King Tut's tomb infected people a hundred years ago. This theory, though, does suggest that people who warned of death by poisons might not have been so far off.

Ultimately, unless new science becomes available to us, we may never know if the many deaths after the opening of King Tut's tomb were connected. Science offers one possible explanation in the form of Aspergillus, but there are things even science can't explain.

The mysteries surrounding King Tut live on. Some archaeologists now speculate that his hasty burial meant that he was placed in the front rooms of another, even richer burial chamber of a family member. They think the missing burial of Queen Nefertiti could be behind one of the walls of King Tut's tomb. If so, it probably contains even more splendid treasures. And perhaps another curse—or an unknown bacteria or fungus that could threaten once again to punish those who disturb the dead.

CHAPTER SIX

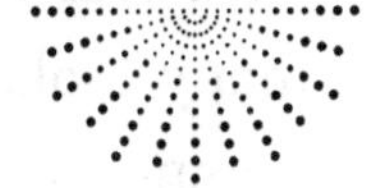

The Vanished Pilot

She is probably the most famous missing person in the world. Some think they have found her bones on a tiny island in the Pacific Ocean. Others think she rests deep beneath the sea, the shadowy remains of her airplane captured on faint radar images. And some think she survived to live out another life altogether.

But even if she hadn't gone missing trying to be the first woman to fly around the globe, Amelia Earhart would be remembered for her courage and her adventurous spirit.

Amelia Earhart was always a daredevil. As a little girl in the early 1900s, she built a homemade rollercoaster out of wood in her backyard. When World War I broke out, she took a break from college to become a nurse so she wouldn't feel "useless." Watching the WWI pilots train sparked her first interest in airplanes.

In her book *20 Hours 40 Minutes*, she wrote, "...when the snow blown back by the propellers stung my face[,] I felt a first urge to fly. I tried to get permission to go up, but the rules forbade."

After the horrors of World War I and the devastation of the Influenza Pandemic, many looked to the future in the Roaring Twenties. White women across the United States gained the right to vote in 1920, after decades of fighting for this basic freedom. During the war, women had proven that they could treat wounded men under fire, drive ambulances across battlefields, and serve as spies. Many women were anxious to prove that they were capable of anything men could do, and Amelia Earhart was among them.

Following World War I, "barnstormer" pilots traveled the United States performing tricks in their airplanes, including racing, doing various whirls and loops through the air, and sometimes even carrying gymnasts to do tricks on the wings. Many of the barnstormers had been pilots in World War I. They enjoyed the thrill of flying and were looking for a way to support their aviation by doing stunts and air meets or races.

The barnstormers caught Earhart's attention, especially because they offered airplane rides to onlookers. Amelia didn't have the money to continue college, but when she took her first airplane ride in 1920, she said in *The Fun of It*, "As soon as we left the ground, I knew I myself had to fly."

She worked multiple jobs to save the money for flying lessons and walked four miles from the last bus stop to reach the flying field for each lesson from pioneering female pilot Neta Snook. In 1910, several female pilots in Europe had earned pilot's licenses, and throughout the decade women around the world proved themselves capable of flying as stunt pilots, spies, and even in combat. A German woman, Katharins Paulus, even invented the first modern parachute. So, Amelia joined a small but determined group of female pilots.

Amelia Earhart during her early flying years. Image from 20 Hours 40 Minutes *and Wikimedia.*

Even when financial problems forced Amelia to sell her first plane, she didn't give up her love of flying. She wrote about her flight experiences, which opened up new opportunities for her as she became a voice for female pilots. In 1928, she was invited to be the first woman to fly across the Atlantic from the United States to the United Kingdom—as a flight recorder and passenger.

In the logbook on the flight, she wrote, "The view is too vast and lovely for words. I think I am happy... kneeling here at the table gulping beauty... A night of stars. North the horizon is clear cut. To the south it is a smudge. The exhausts send out glowing meteors. How marvellous is a machine and the mind that made it."

As the flights' fuel ran low, they touched down in Wales in the United Kingdom. Earhart was determined to make the flight again someday on her own.

Her involvement in the flight and her public appearances gave her more opportunities to fly. In 1932, she fulfilled her goal of flying across the Atlantic Ocean solo—the first woman to do so. She participated in air races and exhibitions and encouraged other women to fly. Then in 1935, she was the first woman to fly solo from Hawaii to the Continental United States—an even longer and more dangerous journey.

In *Last Flight*, a collection of Earhart's messages, she reported on her first flight across the Pacific, "Stars hung outside my cockpit window near enough to touch. I have never seen so many or such large ones. I shall never forget the contrast of the white clouds and the moonlight and the starlight against the black of the sea."

Earhart had one last goal she longed to accomplish: become the first woman to fly around the world. Her husband, publisher George Putnam, recorded in *Last Flight* that she told him, "Please don't be concerned. It just seems that I must try this flight. I've weighed it all carefully. With it behind me life will be fuller and richer. I can be content. Afterward it will be fun to grow old."

It wasn't that Earhart didn't feel worry or fear, but once she had decided something, she didn't let fear stop her. She knew the flight was dangerous. She wanted to do it as close to the equator as possible to make it the longest flight around the world by any pilot—male or female. She tried to start on such a journey in early 1937 with a new plane—a Lockheed Electra—and two navigators, but the wheels failed when she tried to take off and she didn't even get off the ground. Earhart saw failure as a challenge, not a dead end.

Amelia Earhart in front of the special Electra she would take around the world. Image courtesy of NASA.

A few months later, she tried again, accompanied by navigator Fred Noonan. His life is a bit of a mystery to go with his death. He was born either in Ireland or the United States, and he had worked at sea since he was thirteen, becoming a ship's captain before getting his pilot's license. We don't have many details of his life, but he had decades of experience navigating by sea and air, especially in the dangerous stretch over the Pacific Ocean. He even charted the routes that Pan Am Airway's planes would take when flying over the Pacific, so he seemed like an ideal choice for Earhart's navigator.

Earhart and Noonan flew the Electra from California to Florida, and from there headed off around the world.

Earhart skirted down along the Caribbean and Latin America to Brazil. From there, she crossed the Atlantic to Africa and over the Sahara Desert. She flew past the Arabian Peninsula and to India and then across the South Pacific.

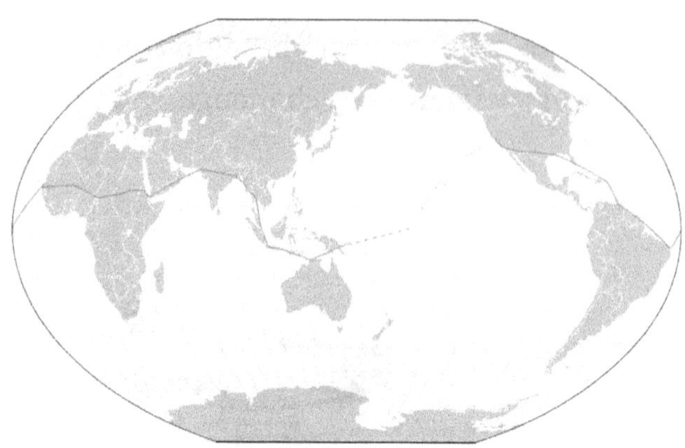

Earhart and Noonan's route around the world. Image courtesy Hellerick via Wikimedia license CC-BY-SA 3.0.

Now before her was the longest and most difficult stretch of ocean: the wide expanse of the Pacific Ocean where there were few places she might stop if her plane had engine trouble or ran low on fuel.

Earhart and Noonan took off from Papua New Guinea with the Electra heavy—almost overloaded—with fuel. Fuel was the deciding factor in their success because planes at the time could not carry enough gasoline to cross the Pacific without stopping. Their goal was Howland Island between Papua New Guinea and Hawaii where they could refill their tanks. Howland Island is hardly more than 15 feet above the ocean and difficult to locate in the best of circumstances. A United States ship, the *Itasca*, was waiting to help guide them to the island, a tiny speck against the wide, relentless sea.

In *Last Flight*, Earhart recorded thinking on a different flight, "The possibility of one little airplane and one little ship passing near enough to see each other in that rather large ocean seemed ridiculous."

Now, on July 2, 1937, Earhart and Noonan's lives depended on that ridiculous possibility. But something went wrong with their communication system. The *Itasca* could hear Earhart, but she could not hear them. Some speculate the Electra's antenna was damaged taking off from Papua New Guinea because of the weight of the fuel.

Earhart requested that the *Itasca* try to hone in on their radio transmission to find and guide them. She whistled to give them a constant signal, but the *Itasca* couldn't lock on the frequency Earhart was using. They sent her Morse Code, trying to communicate or help her to find her way, but she couldn't lock in on that signal either. She reported that their course should take them directly over Howland Island, but she could not see the island or the *Itacsa*.

Earhart reported, "We are on the line 157-337."

Then, the Electra went silent.

That "one little airplane" was lost in the "rather large ocean."

Radio operators around the Pacific continued to pick up faint signals that may have come from the Electra, but they could not trace the plane or Earhart and Noonan. The United States launched the largest manhunt in its history up to that point, but the Pacific Ocean is vast, and it seemed to have swallowed the little plane. The *Itasca* was not well prepared for a rescue mission. There was confusion over Earhart's last location because many of the officers were on the island preparing for the welcome party instead of on the ship tracking her messages. This may have led the search party to look in the wrong direction.

On July 19th, 1937, the search ended and Amelia Earhart

and Fred Noonan were declared missing, and then declared dead two years later.

Earhart and Noonan before their fateful flight. Image courtesy of the San Diego Air and Space Museum Archive.

What happened to Amelia Earhart and Fred Noonan?

The most likely explanation is that the plane ran out of fuel and Earhart crashed into the ocean. Earhart and Noonan may have died on impact. Earhart had once told her husband, recorded in *Last Flight*, "When I go, I'd like best to go in my plane. Quickly." Noonan may not have felt the same, but without fuel, they had little choice.

But Earhart, Noonan, or both could have survived a crash into the ocean. The plane would have gone nose-first, pulled forward by the weight of the engine, but those empty fuel tanks may have helped them to float a little while before the plane went under. They had a raft and other emergency equipment, so it's possible they survived a crash landing in the ocean only to drift, either dying at sea or becoming castaways on some Pacific island.

Some explorers are using radar to search the sea floor for the lost plane. They made headlines when they found an object that looks like the Electra, but it turned out to be a plane-shaped rock formation. Many planes crashed in the Pacific during World War II, shortly after Earhart went missing, making it even more challenging to find the Electra, but these searchers are determined to keep looking.

An alternate theory suggests that Noonan and Earhart searched for a different island to land on when they realized they were out of fuel and couldn't find Howland.

An argument for this idea is that for about a week after the crash, radio operators on the *Itasca* and around the Pacific heard weak radio signals that may have come from the Electra. They were on the radio channel used by American pilots and included the faint sound of a human voice and "dashes," or long beeps. Noonan knew Morse Code, but Earhart didn't, so if he was too badly injured to use the radio, she might have been trying to signal with the long beeps. Unfortunately, hoaxers desperate for attention during the search pretended to be Earhart or to know something about her location, and other countries had their own radio operations and codes, so that makes it more difficult to sort all of the signals.

In 1940, human bones were found on an island 300 miles from Howland called Nikumaroro or Gardner Island. The bones are now missing, but the measurements taken of them are a close match for Earhart's measurements. Shoes have also been found on the island that appear to belong to a man and a woman and to have been made in the 1930s, along with a few other artifacts, but we don't know how they ended up on the island—whether because Earhart and Noonan crashed there or the artifacts washed up on shore from someone and somewhere else. A recently discovered skull fragment that may have come from the island is being tested for a DNA match to Earhart's family. Researchers are also studying a patch of aluminum found on the island for any hints it could have come from the Electra.

Are both hypotheses possible? Could we have found Earhart's plane and the place where her rescue raft came to rest after she drifted at sea? That's possible, but only if the radio transmissions are fake, because the radio needed power from the plane to continue working.

Adding another twist to the mystery, the people of Mili Atoll in the Marshall Islands tell stories about a white man and woman who crashed their plane on the island long ago. Many believe this may have been Earhart and Noonan, especially because there were few women flying at the time as pilots or passengers.

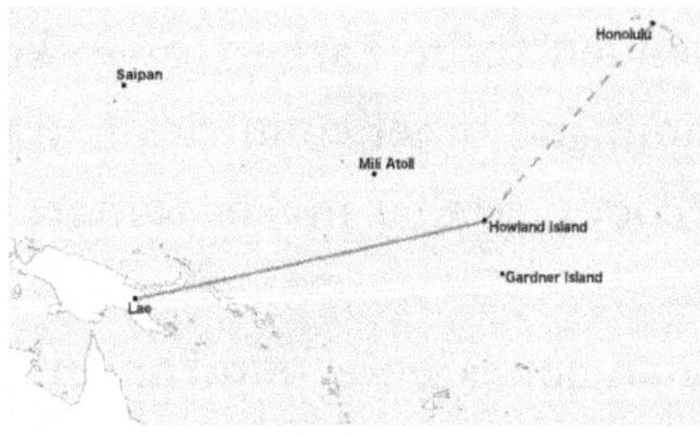

A map showing Earhart's planned route from Lae, Papua New Guinea to Howland Island. The dotted line shows how she should have reached Honolulu, Hawaii. Possible crash sites include Mili Atoll in the Marshall Islands and Gardner Island, another name for Nikumaroro Island. Image courtesy of snowfire via Wikimedia license CC BY 4.0.

According to the story, the two were eventually captured by the Japanese, who controlled the island at the time. This was in the lead-up to World War II, and it's possible the Japanese thought they were valuable prisoners. Earhart and Noonan likely would have died in a Japanese prison camp, though some think Earhart escaped and started a new life—though without any solid reason or proof she would do this.

Earhart sleuths found pieces of metal on the island that could have come from the Electra, and a few photos have surfaced in various locations after 1937 that show someone who looked like Earhart, but none have been verified to be her.

Some have even suggested Amelia Earhart was sent to spy on the Japanese for the US government, or that she was forced to become a "Tokyo Rose," the English-speaking women who sent broadcasts to American troops in the Pacific to demoralize them and help the Japanese. Earhart's husband George Putnam listened to many of the Tokyo Rose recording, hoping to hear his wife's voice, but he never did. If the Japanese government or military knew anything about Amelia Earhart's fate, they haven't admitted it.

Until we find the Electra, it will be hard to even guess what happened to Amelia Earhart. The most important thing about Earhart, though, is not that she disappeared, but everything that she did before that fateful day.

CHAPTER SEVEN

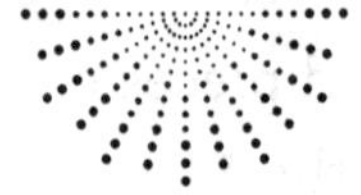

Lost Nazi Plunder

The reign of the Nazi Party in Germany during World War II was one of the darkest hours of the twentieth century. Determined to expand and remake Germany after its losses in World War I, the Nazis planned for a new German Empire reaching across Europe and ruled by those they saw as superior. To them, this meant blond-haired, blue-eyed, healthy and athletic, and of course ready to agree with everything the Nazi Party said. The Nazis oppressed and murdered many of their own citizens, invaded neighboring countries, and tried to wipe out or imprison anyone who was different from their ideal. The Jewish population of Europe was hit especially hard. Nazis drove tens of millions of Jews from their homes and murdered at least six million Jews.

The Nazis didn't just kill people. They also tried to kill cultures and ideas they didn't like. That included literature, music, and art. The Nazi armies stole artwork from countries that they occupied. This is not unusual in conquering armies, but the Nazis did it on a huge scale. They destroyed art that didn't fit with their ideal, kept many famous pieces for their personal collections, and seized their favorite artwork for a grand museum that Nazi leader Adolf Hitler dreamed of building to honor himself and Germany. While many people view priceless and ancient works of art as belonging to all of humanity, the Nazis wanted it all for themselves.

US President Franklin D Roosevelt said, "Today [the paintings] are not only works of art. Today they are the symbols of the human spirit, and of the world the freedom of the human spirit made..." (quoted in *Monuments Men*).

The Mona Lisa *by Renaissance artist Leonardo da Vinci is one of the artworks the Nazis wanted but never managed to steal. Image courtesy of Wikimedia.*

The Allied forces fighting the Nazis, including the Americans, British, and French, sent in art historians and museum curators as Monuments Men (and a few Monuments Women) to help save historical treasures from the Nazis. The Monuments Men snuck the *Mona Lisa* away from the Nazis. They helped stabilize ancient Roman buildings and Renaissance art in Italy during the fighting. They rescued many stolen treasures, uncovering loot hidden in secret chambers in the mountain castle of Neuschwanstein and deep in salt mines in Poland. They rescued everything from ancient Egyptian scrolls to the coffins of long-dead German heroes to bags filled with stolen gold.

Allied soldiers with artworks rescued with from the German castle at Neuschwanstein. Image courtesy of the National Archives and Records Administration.

The book *Monuments Men* describes a hidden cavern filled with famous paintings, priceless sculptures, music manuscripts written by Beethoven, carved wooden doors stolen from churches, and religious artifacts decorated with silver, gold, and jewels.

"How much is it worth?" one of the Allied soldiers asked.

"More than either of us could imagine," the Monuments Man responded.

Despite the efforts of the Monuments Men, many treasures plundered by the Nazis remain missing to this day. Trainloads of gold, priceless works of art, and even a room made entirely of amber may still be out there somewhere, just waiting for someone to discover them.

Waging war is expensive, and the Nazi government stole gold and money from banks and from citizens to fund their conquest. When the Allied forces closed in on the Nazis, the Nazi officers often hid the money and gold, hoping to come back for it later. The Nazis were defeated, so unless an individual soldier snuck back to get the riches, that wealth might still be waiting in hiding.

This has led treasure hunters all over Europe to search for Nazi gold.

A Nazi-era map shows that gold and jewels may have been buried near the Dutch town of Ommeren. Some of the landmarks that existed in the 1940s are now gone, though, so the exact location of the buried treasure is unclear. This has been a headache for the residents of the town, with treasure hunters digging everywhere—including in people's yards and gardens. So far, nothing has been discovered, and Ommeren has asked people to please stop digging up their town. It's possible that someone found the treasure earlier and kept it quiet—or that the treasure is still hidden somewhere nearby.

This kind of search has its risks, though, because gold isn't the only thing the Nazis may have left behind. Smithsonian Magazine quotes a BBC warning that, "there is a real risk of amateur excavators hitting unexploded World War II grenades, bombs or landmines." So, if you do go searching for buried Nazi gold, be very careful, and don't dig up anyone's garden without asking!

A legend of a Nazi gold train persists in Poland. The train supposedly holds stolen gold that left one train station but never arrived at the next, having been hidden somewhere along the way. The idea isn't unreasonable. Rose Valland, a museum worker and spy for the French Resistance, was able to save thousands of French artworks and stolen Jewish belongings when the Nazis hid them on a train fleeing Paris for Germany. She alerted the French Resistance so they could delay the train until the Allied Forces arrived to rescue the stolen artwork. If not, all those treasures might also have disappeared.

The region of Poland with the alleged "gold train," Lower Silesia, had been part of Germany. The Nazis had even started a secret work there called Project Reise, including underground tunnels and bunkers built by prisoners from the concentration camps. When the Soviets moved in at the end of the war, the Germans fled, leaving the mysterious project unfinished. The Poles who later moved into the region found jewels and money buried in jars in their gardens or in the walls of houses—wealth left behind by Germans who hoped to return.

The New Yorker reported on an interview with a former Nazi officer who admitted, "The gold was stored at the police headquarters... The chests were made of iron and hermetically closed with rubber seals. Also the chests were unmarked so nobody would know what's inside."

The region is full of caverns and mines like the one where the Monuments Men found the stolen artwork. Many believe the Germans hid the gold train somewhere in the area, where it waits in the darkness with its treasures.

The Monuments Men found some of the art the Nazis hid in mines, but there may be more left to discover. Image courtesy of the National Archives and Records Administration.

Historians and treasure hunters have scoured the region on foot and with ground-penetrating radar, hoping to find the lost train. So far, they haven't discovered it, but with miles of caverns and tunnels, they believe it's only a matter of time and patience before they bring the train's treasures to light.

Instead of or in addition to a gold train, it's also possible that the region contains a vast buried treasure. A recently discovered Nazi diary suggests that billions of dollars worth of gold taken from a bank was hidden down a well near an old palace in the area. The Polish government is verifying that the diary is authentic, but the owners of the palace plan to restore the building and search for the gold in the process.

You don't have to go to Poland or anywhere in Europe to find lost Nazi treasure. That's because many of the treasures stolen by the Nazis were much smaller than a train: artwork, religious objects, and other priceless artifacts taken from churches, museums, and Jewish prisoners.

In the final days of the war, the Nazis tried to ship some of their resources, including artwork, overseas. Some Latin American countries remained neutral during the war. Nazis escaping the Allied forces fled for these countries. Not all of them made it. American ships sank one Nazi vessel, the SS *Rio Grande*, off the coast of Brazil. It rested there for decades. As the ship has come apart over time, crates of rubber meant for the war effort have floated free and washed up on beaches in Florida, Texas, and Brazil. Aside from rubber, other Nazis treasures may still surface from Nazi shipwrecks.

Some of the Nazi's stolen artwork went into private collections, either sold to help fund the war or kept by the Nazis and their families. Sometimes collectors or museums find paintings and other art that no one remembered was stolen. In 2012, German officials investigating the son of a Nazi-era art dealer for alleged tax evasion discovered a collection of 1,500 missing works of art, including paintings by Monet, Renoir, and Matisse. Despite these finds, there are still hundreds of lost artworks out there waiting to be discovered.

The Amber Room may be the most famous of the lost Nazi treasures. Amber is a gem or precious mineral made of fossilized resin or sap from trees that lived millions of years ago. It's usually a caramel or golden color, and is mostly found around the Baltic region of northern Europe. The

Amber Room was a room decorated with six tons of amber along with gold leafing and other gems. It was originally built in Prussia (now part of Germany and Poland). The Prussian king gifted it to the Russian Tsar Peter the Great, and the panels of the Amber Room moved to Russia, ending up in the Catherine Palace. The glittering room was called the "Eighth Wonder of the World."

The Amber Room was a priceless work of art. Image courtesy of Andrey Zeest and Wikimedia.

When the Nazis invaded Russia, the curators of the Amber Room tried to move it or hide it behind wallpaper. When the Nazis reached the Catherine Palace, they quickly found the room and took the panels to Germany. There, the panels were reassembled in a castle, and German museum director Alfred Rohde became their guardian. In 1943, he was advised to pack up the panels for safety. In 1944, the Soviets bombed the castle where the panels had been stored.

And that is the last we know for certain of the Amber Room. Some people think Rohde never moved the panels and they were destroyed in the bombing. One investigator claimed to have found what looked like pieces of some of the non-amber stone mosaics from the Amber Room in the ruins of the bombed city. The panels also may have been hidden near the castle, or shipped away and hidden elsewhere. Some who were in the city claimed they saw it loaded on a German ship that sank. Divers have searched the wreckage of the ship, but they found no evidence of the Amber Room on the wreckage. Though, if the pieces were on a different ship, they may have ended up elsewhere.

There have been strange occurrences related to the hunt for the Amber Room. A former German soldier who was investigating what had happened to the Amber Room was murdered in the forest in 1987. His murderer was never identified or captured. And in 1992, a Soviet general who had been speaking to a reporter about the Amber Room died in a suspicious car accident. It seemed perhaps someone knew the Amber Room's secret and didn't want the answers found.

The Amber Room's story doesn't end there. In 1997, a German man tried to sell a piece of mosaic art. Police and investigators immediately swarmed him. The mosaic he was trying to sell was a part of the Amber Room, though he claimed he didn't know anything about its identity or where it came from. His father had been a German soldier in World War II and must have stolen or been given the mosaic at some point. It remains a tantalizing hint that more pieces of the Amber Room may be waiting to be discovered.

It's not only about the value of all that precious stone and gold. The true wealth of these treasures lies in their beauty and history. Even in the darkness and destruction of World War II, people fought and died to save the things that were still good in the world. Monuments Man Ronald

Balfour (quoted in *Monuments Men*) said, "If these things are lost or broken or destroyed, we lose a valuable part of our knowledge about our forefathers. No age lives entirely alone; every civilization is formed not merely by its own achievements but by what it has inherited from the past. If these things are destroyed, we have lost a part of our past, and we shall be the poorer for it."

Portrait of a Young Man *by Renaissance painter Raphael is one of the pieces of art still missing from the Nazi plunder of Europe. There is a $25,000 (US) reward for information leading to its recovery.*

CHAPTER EIGHT

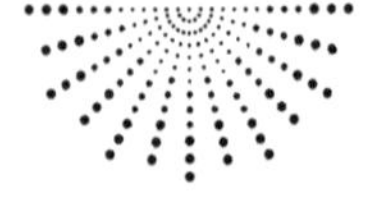

The Death of Mr. Drum

Do you think it's important to tell the truth? What if people say you're lying anyway? What if they're willing to kill you for speaking up?

On December 31, 1957, a Black journalist known as Mr. Drum made his way through Sophiatown, the segregated Black neighborhood outside the capital of South Africa. The neighborhood wasn't always safe, but he wasn't afraid. As a journalist and a young father, he was on a mission to uncover the hidden abuses of the government against its native African citizens. That New Year's Eve, he was in the process of investigating a crooked doctor whose patients died of botched surgeries. Mr. Drum had previously written news stories revealing secrets about farms, prisons, gangs, and the government. As Mr. Drum walked down the street, an unknown man leaped out and stabbed him several times.

Mr. Drum's friend and fellow journalist Daniel Can Themba, quoted in *Literary Journalism Studies,* described the scene he saw in the morning, with Mr. Drum, "lying on the green grass, one shoe off, one arm twisted behind, the head pressed against the ground, the eyes glazed in sightless death." Themba said footprints on the ground showed that Mr. Drum had struggled and tried to escape.

The killer was probably a hired criminal, so as Mr. Drum bled to death, he likely never knew which of his many enemies tried to silence the truth.

With government leaders unwilling to investigate the death, Mr. Drum's murderer escaped justice, but by looking at Mr. Drum's world and his investigations, we find the most likely suspects.

Mr. Drum's real name was Henry Nxumalo. He was born in South Africa in 1917. At that time, his country had only recently gained the right to have its own government after being a colony controlled by the Dutch and then the British. Many Black South Africans did not have opportunities for education or careers. The colonial-era laws allowed only White people to work in the government, vote, or own land in most of the country and put many restrictions on non-White people, including the native Black Africans.

Henry's parents were able to send him to a school run by Christian missionaries who would educate people regardless of race. Henry did well in school and showed great promise as a writer. When World War II broke out, Henry joined the army, which allowed him to travel to other parts of Africa and to Europe.

After the war, Henry and other Black South Africans were ready to take a bigger role in their nation. Many of them moved to cities looking for work and demanded more rights. After all, they lived and worked in the nation, too, and had even fought for their country in the war. In many parts of the world, the years following World War II led to more civil rights for ethnic minorities and other oppressed people. For instance, Mahatma Gandhi pioneered peaceful protests against British rule of India until he was murdered in 1948, and Martin Luther King, Jr. began his advocacy for racial reforms in the United States in the 1950s.

This South African sign reinforcing segregation is in English and Afrikaans, two of the languages of South Africa. Image courtesy of Wikimedia.

Yet in response to Black demands for more rights in South Africa, the majority of the White voting population enacted rules of segregation called apartheid, a South African word meaning “apart-ness.” Blacks couldn’t get a passport to leave the country. They weren't allowed to travel to White parts of the city or country unless they were working for White people there, and they had to have passes to travel and follow curfews. A Black person could not be a boss over a White person. Beaches, schools, restaurants, hotels, sports, hospitals, and even most churches were segregated. The government spent much less money on Black institutions than White ones, but it put heavier taxes on the Black population. With all this happening, the South African government tried to convince the world that its Black citizens were happy and free.

Henry Nxumalo wanted to use his writing skills to tell the real stories about what was happening in his country. But Whites owned all the newspapers and rarely hired Black reporters, and no serious newspapers were available for Black readers. The only exception was *Drum* magazine. It was founded by a White South African, Jim Bailey, a former World War II fighter pilot whose father had made a fortune in South African diamonds. Bailey was bothered by apartheid and wanted a magazine for Black South Africans. Because of the apartheid laws, White men had to be the chief editors for *Drum*, and some of the reporters and photojournalists were also White, but Henry Nxumalo quickly became *Drum*'s star reporter.

The logo for Drum magazine. Image courtesy of Wikimedia.

It was dangerous for Nxumalo to write about the truth, but it was even more dangerous to live in a society where his people—his family and children—were treated so badly. He set out to uncover the secrets of South Africa's apartheid, writing under the name Mr. Drum.

Nxumalo had heard that White farmers abused their Black workers, forcing children to work, tricking men into signing bad contracts, and working the laborers to death. The farmers denied this. So, Nxumalo used a false name and got jobs at several farms.

Nxumalo wrote of working until he was exhausted, and how the farmers hit him. He heard stories of Black workers beaten to death and others who froze trying to survive in the filthy, jail-like housing. The Henry Nxumalo Foundation reports that when Nxumalo said he wanted to leave, one farmer took his pass—required for Black men to travel—and tore it to pieces.

"On this farm you don't just quit when you want to," the farmer said. "Now you can't leave without my permission. I can have you arrested..."

Nxumalo escaped from the farm at night—a crime which he could have been shot for.

He then went to another farm. *The Journalist* project quotes his experience with that farmer: "He told me that if Jantjie [an overseer] complained about my work tomorrow he would beat me up and then have me arrested. He clapped [slapped] me on the left cheek with his open right hand and told me to face the wall. Then he kicked me between the legs three times with his boot. I shuddered with the pain."

Mr. Drum escaped to tell his stories. This led to a boycott

of South African potatoes and outrage around the world; thanks to its brave and innovative stories, *Drum* was no longer a magazine only for South Africa—it was read across Africa and the world.

The racism and segregation in South Africa led many Black South Africans to protest and demand better treatment. Image courtesy of Paul Weinberg license CC-BY-SA 2.0.

For his next big expose, Nxumalo wanted to go inside the Black prisons to show how the officials abused the prisoners there. The only way to do that was to be arrested. It was illegal for Black men to wander the city without a pass, so that was exactly what Nxumalo did. He pretended to be drunk and wandered in front of the police offices. When the police didn't notice him, he broke a window to make certain they did. That got him thrown in prison for five days. While there, he documented how the guards beat and humiliated the prisoners, such as making them dance naked to ensure they didn't have anything hidden on their bodies.

Nxumalo's article "Mr. Drum Goes to Jail," reprinted in *The South African Reader: History Culture Politics*, told the world, "Many of us who were going to prison for the first time didn't know exactly where the reception office was. Although the prison officials were with us, no one was directing us. But if a prisoner hesitated, slackened his half--running pace and looked round, he got a hard boot kick on the buttocks, a slap on his face or a whipping from the warders."

One elderly man was slow and confused, so a guard, "...hit him with his open hand on the temples and told him to wake up."

A photojournalist for *Drum* pretended to do a photo shoot near the prison so he could sneak pictures for the story.

This story also produced an uproar. In this case, the government responded with a new law—which made it illegal to spread "false" information about prisons. They claimed Mr. Drum was lying, despite the story and photos he presented as proof. The government wasn't willing to acknowledge the truth about its prisons, but the world now knew thanks to Mr. Drum.

Henry Nxumalo was opening the world's eyes to the conditions in South Africa's apartheid, and the government was taking notice of his work and that of other people trying to change the oppression and unfairness in South Africa.

And that was when someone had Nxumalo killed. At the time, Nxumalo was working on a new investigation into a White doctor called Dr. Big who performed illegal operations on Black patients. Some of those patients later died. The doctor was an influential man and was friendly with the police in Sophiatown. Many people thought the doctor, perhaps along with the police, silenced "Mr. Drum" before he could write his story.

The murder also could have been committed out of revenge. Nxumalo had named the farmers whose abuses he endured while undercover, such as the overseer Jantjie and the farm owner Snyman. His story cost them their reputation and money when people boycotted their farms, and they were wealthy and powerful men. One of the farmers might have decided to get even with Nxumalo.

The government had taken notice of Mr. Drum, too. It had passed a law just to counter his efforts to expose the truth about the prison system. The apartheid government sometimes ordered police to kill demonstrators, and some people who approved of segregation and apartheid used violence and even murder to support the regime. One of them could have ended Mr. Drum's life.

Henry Nxumalo had made a lot of enemies. He had also written about the gangs in Sophiatown called Tsotsis. Sometimes the Tsotsi members celebrated Nxumalo, such as when he wrote about the abuse in the prisons. Other times, though, he made gang members angry by describing their violent and illegal activities and calling for police to clean up the streets. It's possible the gangs or even an individual gang member decided Mr. Drum had to die.

Later rumors said a criminal was paid to stab Mr. Drum, but no one ever answered the question of who was behind the death of Henry Nxumalo. The police had no interest in investigating the murder, and it was swept under the rug.

Mr. Drum's legacy lived on, however. His friend and fellow writer and "*Drum* boy" Can Themba was quoted in

The Journalist project saying, "...dear Henry, Mr Drum is not dead. Indeed, even while you lived others were practising the game of Mr Drum. Now we shall take over where you left off."

The South African government cleared out Sophiatown and destroyed it as punishment against its residents for demanding to be treated fairly. *Drum* magazine documented the action so the world could see what was happening in South Africa. *Drum* also covered the Sharpeville Massacre, when the South African police fired into a group of unarmed protesters, killing 69 and injuring almost two hundred others, including women and children. It also helped give a voice to civil rights activist Nelson Mandela, who was arrested for his fight against apartheid.

Nelson Mandela was an important anti-apartheid leader and later president of South Africa. Image courtesy of the National Archives and Records Administration.

Because of the attention brought to the atrocities of the South African government by *Drum* and later media, other countries started to place boycotts and restrictions on the South African government until they offered freedom for all of South Africa's citizens. Finally, in 1990, South Africa repealed apartheid and held free elections. Nelson Mandela won in a landslide and became the first Black president of South Africa.

Mr. Drum would have been pleased that his children and now grandchildren finally had their freedom, though the changes came more than 30 years after his murder. His daughter Suzette also became a journalist and wrote against apartheid like her father.

She told *The Journalist* project, "I believe strongly that his killing was payback for exposing the injustices of the system. Knowing this made me love him even more, and feel even more upset at losing him... There is a need for journalists to be courageous and spirited. They need to pursue their course with all they have, no matter the risk to their life and their well being."

CHAPTER NINE

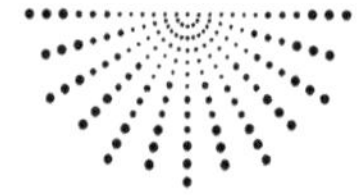

The Dead Mountain Ski Party

In late February 1959, a rescue party set out into the wintery Russian wilderness. They were searching for nine experienced college-aged skiers who had gone on a cross-country trip weeks earlier and never returned. Their destination: Kholat Syakhl, or Dead Mountain, in the northern Ural Mountains near Siberia. On their journey, the rescue party saw bright lights flashing in the sky, giving them a sense of foreboding.

When the search party finally found the skiers' tent, it was partly collapsed with snow gathered on top, but everything inside was orderly: boots by the tent door, wood chopped for the camping stove, diaries and cameras tucked into place.

The rescue party examining the Dyatlov group's tent.
Image courtesy of Wikimedia.

The BBC reported an interview with one of the searchers who remembers finding food, "...sliced up as if they were getting ready to have supper or something and didn't have time."

The canvas tent had been cut open—from the inside, according to analysis of the torn fibers—and everyone had vanished.

Rescuers found footprints leading away from the tent. It had been so cold that night that when the skiers' warm feet hit the snow it melted and instantly refroze into eight or nine pairs of icy tracks, which clearly showed feet that were bare or in socks. It appeared that the skiers had fled from their tent in a panic, slicing their way free rather than using the door and rushing underdressed into the bitter snow. They left behind knives and axes that could have been used as weapons or tools. But why?

The search party continued to scour the areas for signs of the missing skiers. About one mile (one and a half kilometers) from the tent, they discovered a stand of trees and a circle of blackened wood and ash: a fire pit. Bits of burned clothing littered the area. One of the large trees overhead had many broken limbs as though one or more people had tried to climb high into the branches. And under the snow near the fire pit and large tree, the rescuers found the bodies of two of the skiers.

These two men wore nothing but their winter underclothing. They had burn marks and minor cuts on their skin and clothing but no deadly injuries. They had frozen to death. And after they died, someone had laid them out next to each other in a peaceful pose, as though the dead men only slept under their chilly blanket of snow.

The search party now knew that the Russian winter had claimed at least two of the seven men and two women in the skiing expedition. Rumors claimed the skiers might have been fleeing over the Russian border to travel to America. Unlikely as such an escape was, Russia (at the time part of the USSR or Soviet Union) and the United States of America were in a standoff—a Cold War—and fears of spies and traitors ran high.

The search party had to discover what had happened to the other skiers.

They backtracked toward the tent, checking under the snow with long poles, and found three more bodies. These skiers had collapsed in the snow near each other, all facing toward the tent as if they were trying to return. If so, they fell one by one in the attempt. One of the dead was the group's leader, Igor Dyatlov, and another was one of the two women in the group. These bodies wore more clothing than those near the fire. They also showed signs of minor injuries, including scraps and bruises. The third person in this group, another man, had a crack on his skull—an injury to the back of his head. Yet these three, like the first two bodies, appeared to have frozen to death.

Four skiers were still missing. It would be several months before the snow melted enough to uncover their bodies. They were in a low ravine a short distance from the trees. They had warmer clothes than the other skiers. Signs under the snow, like branches laid on the ground, suggest they might have tried to build a shelter.

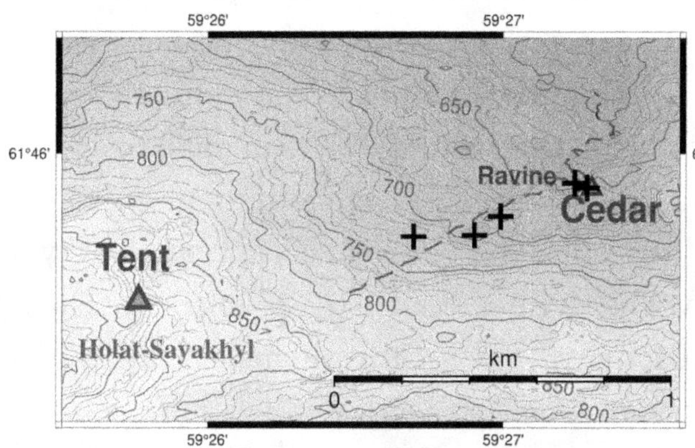

This map shows where the searchers found the bodies. The cedar is the tree where the group made the fire, and where the first two men died. The ravine is close by, and the three crosses show where the three died who appeared to be trying to return to the tent. Image courtesy of Merikanto via Wikimedia license CC-BY-SA 4.0 International.

In fact, this last group in the ravine did not freeze to death. They died of blunt force injuries, the equivalent of being hit by a fast-moving car. Their rib cages or skulls had been smashed, though they had no signs of serious external injuries: no cuts or bleeding. It appeared some inhuman force had smashed their bones while they huddled against the cold. Their faces were also damaged, but no one knows if this happened before or after their deaths. Whatever killed them has never been identified. Their official cause of death was, "compelling natural force." That's a fancy way to say, "We don't know, but it was powerful—too powerful to be the work of a human."

This last group of skiers had one more odd clue: a sweater. The second woman in the expedition died with this last group, and she wore a sweater that belonged to one of the two men found under the tree. It's entirely reasonable to imagine that when the first two men died, their friends laid them out and took their extra clothing to try to survive, so wearing the other man's sweater isn't necessarily a sign of foul play. The sweater itself is the problem: it tested positive for radioactivity. A few other items of clothing from the group in the ravine also had lower levels of radioactivity, but none was found on any of the other skiers.

There were no survivors of the Dyatlov expedition to Dead Mountain, so we can only guess what happened that February night. A tenth member of the party, Yuri Yudin, had to turn back just after the group started because of severe pain in his legs, which saved his life. He said the group was well prepared for the trip and wasn't having any personal problems.

The group's last journal entry is for January 31st, just a few days after they began their cross-country skiing. It mentions minor arguments about who had to sleep closest to the fire and problems with their skis, as well as time spent singing and talking about life and love—nothing that sounds unusual for a group of college students having an adventure. The cameras had pictures of the group skiing, laughing, and working together. The last picture is from February 1st, presumably the night the skiers died, and shows the group digging a level area in the snow to set up their tent.

Yet later that night, they cut a hole in the side of the tent and fled, leaving behind their coats and shoes. They probably arrived together at the site on the edge of the trees where they started the fire, since they later shared the clothes of the men who froze to death there. We don't know how long they stayed by the trees. Did the group fall asleep by the fire, only to have the first two men freeze? Or did some of the group move around, maybe watching for danger or help, and the two lookouts by the fire froze while the others were away? The two by the fire had burns that would have hurt but not killed them. They might have become disoriented when hypothermia set in, maybe falling into the fire or even taking off their outer clothing as they became so cold they felt hot. Were their friends there when that happened? We only know from the situation of their bodies that someone carefully moved them after they died.

In addition to starting a fire, one or more of the group also climbed the large tree, breaking many branches. This could explain the minor cuts and scrapes on some of their hands and faces, but why did they do it? To collect larger branches? See their camp or something else in the distance? Escape from something that frightened them?

It seems that the group split up after the first two men froze to death. Since there are no signs of injuries on those first victims, there's no reason to suspect anyone killed them. Their friends laid out their bodies and divided up their clothes. Were the survivors unable to keep a fire going? Or were they frightened of staying in that spot? The group might have split up to try to find help, or they might have disagreed over which way to go. Some of the minor injuries on their bodies could have been the result of a fistfight.

There was no correct choice at that point, though. The group of three heading for the tent collapsed of cold and exhaustion and died of hypothermia. The group of four remains the most mysterious. If they fell into the ravine, or if they took shelter and something fell on them, why did it not cause any external injuries?

The ravine group also contains the most mysterious of the skiers: Semyon Zolotaryov. Unlike the others, who were in their early 20s, Zolotaryov was almost 40 and was a veteran of World War II. He joined the expedition at the last minute, and some of the group weren't happy to have a relative stranger with them, but they allowed him along.

Zolotaryov's family later raised questions about his autopsy report. It described his tattoos and other physical features—and the family of Seymon Zolotaryov said the description didn't match the Zolotaryov they knew. In 2018, they petitioned to have his body checked by a private lab to see if his DNA matched theirs. The answer came back: it was not a match. The Russian government ordered a second test and reported that the first test was a mistake and Zolotaryov's DNA *was* a match. The conflicting reports have only led to more questions about the mysterious last-minute member of the expedition.

It's possible Zolotaryov (or someone using his name) may have been sent by the KGB (the Soviet Union's spy agency) to watch the group and make certain they weren't trying to leave the country or meet foreign spies on their journey. Likewise, he might have been a foreign spy himself, using the cover of the trip to engage in espionage. During the Cold War, it was not unusual for the Soviet Union and other governments to spy on their own people. Rumors said that Zolotaryov was carrying a camera and a notepad when his body was found, but these things disappeared during the investigation. Did Zolotaryov have a secret mission on the trip?

Maybe Zolotaryov holds a key to the strangest part of the entire incident: why did the skiers leave the safety of the tent in the first place?

The tent was warm and secure. When the rescue party found it, the only obvious damage was the tear where someone had sliced their way free. What would cause experienced outdoors men and women to abandon the safety of their tent for the freezing Russian winter night? We may never know for certain, but scientists, amateur sleuths, and the family members of the victims have several theories.

The fact that the skiers climbed the tree has led some to suggest they were attacked by someone and were trying to escape.

The investigators first blamed the native Mansi people.

They are local reindeer herders who gave the mountain its name. The Dyatlov journal mentions passing Mansi hunters and describes some of the carvings the Mansi place on trees for guidance, but it doesn't say anything about having trouble with the Mansi. The Dyatlov group would have been the first Russians to trek through the area—it was controlled by the massive Soviet Union but had not been explored thoroughly by outsiders—but there's no evidence the Mansi had anything to do with the skiers. The tent was cut from the inside, the footprints around the tent lacked Mansi boots, and the majority of the skiers froze to death. The Mansi had no means to cause the massive internal injuries that killed the group in the ravine.

The Mansi (on the right) are familiar with the area around "Dead Mountain" and even helped with the search for the missing skiers. Image courtesy of Карагеоргий via Wikimedia.

Some have suggested that Zolotaryov had a violent flashback to World War II and attacked some of his comrades or forced them to march out of the tent. Interestingly, the Dyatlov group died on the night of February 1st to February 2nd, which would be Zolotaryov's birthday—assuming he was the real Zolotaryov. But there's no blood or anything else inside the tent to suggest that the group fought there. It's not impossible that Zolotaryov caused the group to leave the tent, or caused them to split up later, but there's no evidence for it. Perhaps he was simply an army veteran trying to use his wartime experience to keep his comrades alive when he led some of the group toward the ravine.

Some people have also suggested the group was attacked by a Chuchuna, a giant man-ape similar to Bigfoot or the yeti. If so, it did not leave any footprints alongside the very human ones in the snow. Others say that the group was attacked by space aliens—a theory that would be difficult to prove or disprove.

One less supernatural theory is that an avalanche covered the tent door and frightened the group into cutting their way out. The group was not camped near the kind of steep slope where avalanches are common, and the Mansi people who know the area best say that avalanches do not happen there. But there is a special kind of avalanche called a slab avalanche that's possible on gentler slopes. In a slab avalanche, a layer of heavy snow builds up on a layer of weaker snow. Eventually, the top slab collapses and slides over anything beneath it. Because it doesn't involve as much snow as a traditional avalanche, it also blows away quickly.

The snow was deep where the Dyatlov group pitched their tent, and they had to dig down to create a flat space for it. This could have weakened the layers of snow. The winds blew fiercely that night, which might have caused more snow to build into a kind of wave over the tent. Maybe at some point, the snow "wave" or slab cracked and slid into the tent, panicking the skiers into fleeing. Some have even suggested that the slab avalanche could have caused the injuries found in the ravine group. Being hit by a huge slab of snow and crushed against the ground could certainly have caused massive internal injuries. Computer models of the area have shown that such a slab avalanche is possible at the Dyatlov site.

Though a slab avalanche was physically possible, it doesn't explain everything. If the four bodies found in the ravine were crushed by a massive slab of snow and ice, how could they have escaped the tent? Even if their friends helped them out of the tent, why take them all the way to the ravine and leave them there to die of their injuries? And what about the radiation on their clothing?

The wind provides another possible culprit for the skiers' deaths. Some mountain winds can howl with the strength of a hurricane. They wail so ferociously through the peaks and over the snow that they hurt people's ears and even put pressure on their minds, causing irrational behavior. Maybe the maddening shriek of the wind caused the skiers to flee just to escape the terrible noise. Some of their injuries could have been caused by being flung down by the strength of the winds, though this theory doesn't explain why some of the skiers tried to climb the tree.

The effects of sound can be so powerful that it can even be used as a weapon. Yuri Yudin lived until 2013, after the fall of the Soviet Union when some of the secrecy of the past lifted. In his later years, when people asked what he thought became of his friends on their ill-fated trip, he said Dyatlov and the others were too experienced to rush outside unprepared, even in the case of an avalanche. He believed the Soviet Union killed them while testing a secret weapon in the mountains. Many of the family members of the victims believe the same thing. They remember the reports of strange lights in the sky above the mountains that February. They don't see other explanations for the strange behaviors of the skiers or odd details like the radiation.

According to this theory, the weapon might have been a sound weapon, poisonous gas, or a parachute mine that explodes in the air and sends shock waves out to destroy things on the ground. Such weapons could have frightened and confused the skiers into fleeing their tent. A shock wave from a parachute mine also could have caused the type of injuries found in the ravine group. The Dyatlov group had to report their proposed route to the government for approval, but they had strayed a little off course—perhaps into a testing range. If Zolotaryov was a spy, he might have been assigned to watch the results of the test from afar or to keep the group away—in which case he failed.

Of course, if the Soviet Union tested weapons in the Ural Mountains, the Mansi people would have been in danger from the experiments. In fact, for several years after that time, the Mansi were told to stay out of the area and not to drink the local water.

A Mansi woman told the BBC that on that night, "This bright, burning object appeared. It was wider at the front, and narrower at the back, with a tail, and there were sparks flying off it."

It would not have been the first time a Cold War

government tested weapons on its own people. Both the Soviet Union and the United States were guilty of such tests in the 1950s. The United States tested nuclear bombs in the desert of southern Nevada, knowing that the radioactive fallout would drift over the people living in southern Nevada and Utah. Even today, "Downwinders" and their children and grandchildren in Nevada and southern Utah have higher rates of cancer because of these experiments. The Soviet Union conducted its own tests, and it was even more secretive about them. It's no wonder that Yuri and many others suspected that strange deaths were the result of government tests.

Yet others have questioned the weapons test theory. Given how many people would have been involved in covering up such an experiment for so long—especially after the Soviet Union dissolved—they doubt that it would have stayed a secret all this time.

A Russian sleuth told the BBC, "If the young people had been killed by an experiment, there is no way the military would have allowed ordinary civilians, friends of the students, to join the search party on that mountain... one of the soldiers would let it slip before he died to some of his relatives—someone would have said something in drunk company. We live in a country where nobody can keep any secrets."

"What went on up there is hard to say," Dyatlov's younger sister recounted to the BBC. "The families were told, 'You will never know the truth, so stop asking questions.' So what could we do? Don't forget, in those days if they told you to shut up, you would be silent."

Unless new records come forth to give us more details, we may never know if the Dyatlov group was the victim of unexpected natural forces, an attack, or weapons fired by their own government. We only know that death came suddenly and unexpectedly upon them that icy February night on Dead Mountain.

The tombstone of the nine skiers. Image courtesy of Дмитрий Никишин via Wikimedia.

CHAPTER TEN

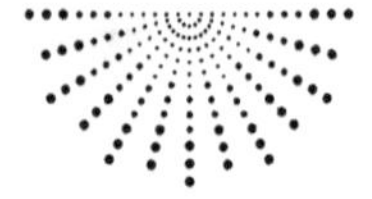

The Fate of the Air Pirates

A US Air Force crew of eight men prepared for a nighttime flight over the Southeast Asian country of Laos on February 4, 1973. This was to be one of their final actions in the Vietnam War, a conflict the United States had entered to prevent communist Soviet Union from expanding its influence in Asia. The sliver of moon had already set and dawn was far away. Patches of clouds blocked the stars. The crew, going by the call sign Baron 52, would slip into the deep darkness over the jungle, hoping to pass over Laos like a ghost.

The Baron 52 crew had gone on many secret flights. Their role in the Vietnam War had been to fly their EC-47 plane on spy missions listening for enemy radio transmissions. This time was different, though. The US had signed the Paris Peace Accords a week earlier, ending US involvement in the Vietnam War and in neighboring countries like Laos. Despite the treaty, the US military ordered the men to spy out the movements of enemy North Vietnamese tanks in Laos. The US plane wasn't supposed to be there, and neither were the tanks. The crew knew this, and at least some of them didn't like it, but they had a duty to follow orders.

The crew of Baron 52 boarded the EC-47. The pilot, co-pilots, and navigators sat in the front of the plane. In the back, the radio operators worked with their top-secret, high-tech electronic equipment. These "back-enders" were experts in spying equipment and decoding messages. The engines coughed out a cloud of bluish smoke, and then the plane roared down the runway and took to the night skies. They quickly rose above 2,000 feet so they and their top secret equipment would be safe from enemy fire. The crew were living their division's motto of, "Unarmed, Alone, Unafraid."

The EC-47 was used for spy missions in the Vietnam War. Image courtesy of the National Museum of the United States Air Force.

During their flight, Baron 52 reported in regularly, every

half an hour. In a radio conversation with another plane, Baron 52 mentioned that they had been targeted by anti-aircraft artillery fire. A short time later, they made their last check-in of "ops normal," not mentioning the artillery. Then, at two o'clock in the morning, the transmissions stopped.

By the time Baron 52 would have run out of gas, they were officially considered missing. Other American planes had begun scanning the ground in hopes of finding the lost plane, but the jungle was thick and the weather turned bad. The first time anyone spotted the crash site, they assumed it was from an older wreck. It took two days to realize it was the Baron 52.

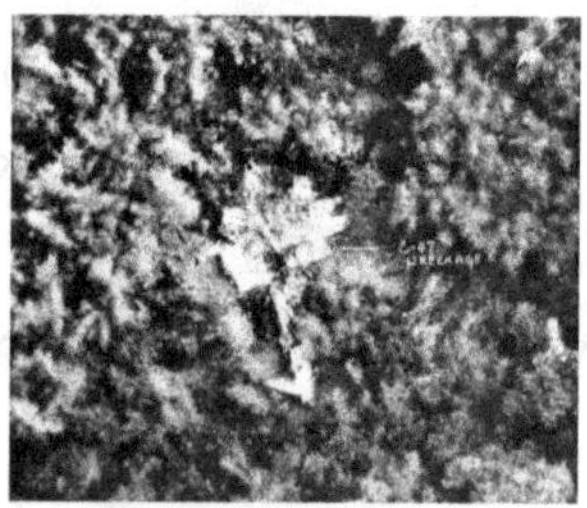

The wreckage of Baron 52 in the jungle. Image courtesy of the United States Air Force and Wikimedia.

Sending out a rescue party proved to be tricky. After all, how do you explain why you need to search for a plane that wasn't supposed to be there in the first place? Four days after the crash, the military sent in rescue helicopters called "Jolly Green Giants" to search for any survivors.

On the way to the crash site, enemy forces shot missiles at the rescue helicopter. The rescuers also spotted "unidentified persons" near the crash site, possibly members of the opposing army. The rescuers were worried they might be going into a trap, but they went forward, even when people shot at them and the helicopter while it hovered over the crash site.

The helicopter lowered the rescue crew down to the jungle floor. The rescuers noted that the plane seemed to have gone straight down, hitting nose first and bouncing over to land on its back, then catching fire. The front part of the plane was smashed and completely destroyed by fire, but the back end was somewhat more intact. The rescuers could see four bodies in the front part of the plane—two strapped into the pilot and co-pilot seats. Whatever had happened, it happened so fast that the pilots hadn't had time to send a distress call or reach for their parachutes. It looked like the plane may have been hit by anti-aircraft artillery, but it was difficult to be certain because the aircraft was so badly damaged. Rescuers didn't try to get inside the plane because of the risk of booby traps set while the wreckage sat in the jungle.

Yet the plane was missing its jump door, which would have allowed the men in the back to parachute to safety. The rescuers' reports don't mention what happened to the top-secret equipment in the back of the plane. The rescue party didn't destroy the remnants of the plane, which they would have done if any top-secret equipment remained, to protect it from enemy soldiers. So, the equipment was probably gone. It could have been saved by one of the back-enders if any survived, but enemy forces also had four days in which to steal it.

There was no time to search for any more clues, not with enemy fire coming from the jungle and the helicopter running low on fuel. The search and rescue crew retrieved the one body they were able to safely remove from the plane and returned to friendly territory.

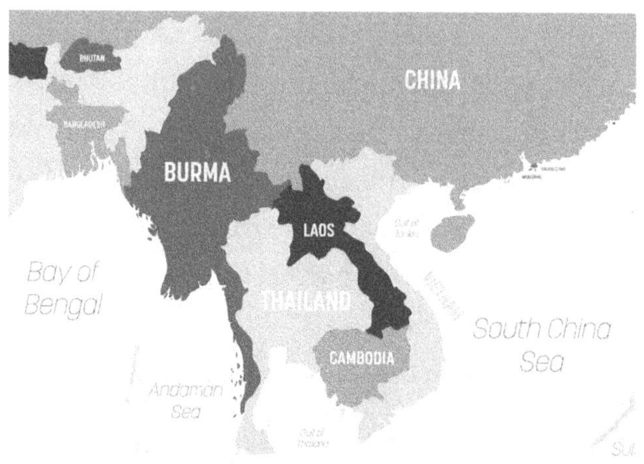

US forces were allowed to be in Thailand, but not in Laos, which stands between Laos and Vietnam on the eastern coast. Image courtesy of pyty via Deposit Photos.

Most of those at the crash site assumed that no one could have survived that landing. But something strange had happened in the meantime. Less than six hours after the crash, American radio operators picked up a message being sent through North Vietnamese channels. The transmission talked about moving four captured "air pirates," "pirate pilots," or "fliers," depending on how the message is translated from Vietnamese.

One translation of the sentence read, "Presently Group 210 has four pirates; they are going to the control of Mr. Van, they are going from 44 to 93, they are having difficulties moving along the road." Another said, "Group 217 is holding four pilots captive, and the group is requesting orders concerning what to do with them..."

We don't know who Group 210 or Group 217 are (possibly the same group translated incorrectly one time), who Mr. Van is, or what 44 and 93 mean. There was a kilometer marker 44 not too far from where Baron 52 crashed. The message also didn't say that the "air pirates" were American, but the North Vietnamese often used "pirate" to describe American military members.

This led to the mystery that endures today: the fate of Baron 52 and the "air pirates."

Following the rescue effort, the US military changed the status of the eight Baron 52 crew members from MIA (missing in action) to KIA (killed in action). Their families, who had been hoping for better news, reacted with sorrow as well as frustration. How would it feel to lose a loved one far away, to be told they were missing and then that they were probably dead—but their bodies had not been found, so you could never be sure?

The mystery is complicated by the feelings in America about the Vietnam War. In earlier wars, most citizens supported the fighting because it felt like self-defense. But many Americans didn't understand why their husbands, brothers, or sons should be drafted and forced to fight against people in a distant country that had never directly attacked the United States. Some families wanted an end to the war so their loved ones could return from fighting or from prisoner of war (POW) camps. Others, however, felt strongly that it was important to stop the Soviet Union from gaining any more power or allies before they became so strong that they would take down the United States as well. Over 50,000 Americans died in the conflict and many more were wounded or permanently disabled, while protesters, counter-protesters, and police in America fought each other over what the war meant for the United States.

These Vietnam veterans protested the US's continued involvement in Vietnam. Image courtesy of Wikimedia.

By the early 1970s, the United States decided to end its official involvement in Vietnam. On January 27, 1973, the United States and North Vietnam signed the Paris Peace Accords. They agreed that the United States would stop fighting and leave within 60 days, and that North Vietnam would free all of its American prisoners of war.

It's possible that neither side kept their promises.

Many in the United States suspected that men listed as "MIA" (missing in action) were actually POWs (prisoners of war). When the US exited Vietnam with the American POWs released by its communist foes, many US families had loved ones still marked as MIA. They wanted answers. Were their relatives actually dead? Or were they suffering in some terrible prison camp in the jungle? The US government didn't press the issue at the time because they didn't want to stir up the fighting again.

Baron 52 was an even trickier situation. Since the US military shouldn't have been spying over Laos, they could hardly ask North Vietnam or Russia, "Hey, did you happen to capture some of our guys on an illegal spy mission?"

So, they said nothing. Or rather, they closed the case. The United States cut off relations with Vietnam and had an ongoing standoff with the Soviet Union, so there was little chance to ask questions about POWs.

Over a thousand MIA Americans never returned from the Vietnam Conflict—alive or dead. Their family members have been asking their own questions ever since. Did those soldiers die in combat? Did they die in a prisoner-of-war camp? Or were they left behind as a sacrifice so the United States could escape the war—especially those in places like Laos that were not officially part of the combat zone?

Rumors and reports of sightings of White POWs in Asia continued to circulate (there were some Black POWs as well, but they were a smaller percentage and not talked about as often).

In 1980, aerial spy photographs of a prison in Laos appeared to show a huge letter "K" and the number "52" etched into the ground—visible from above but not to the prison guards. The letter "K" was supposed to be used as a code for downed American pilots. The "52" could be connected to Baron 52, though the US also had planes called B-52 bombers. The US government didn't know for certain that American POWs were being held at the prison, but they decided to investigate further. Unfortunately, the foreign operatives they hired to check out the site were terrible spies who ruined the secrecy of the mission. If any Americans were at that prison, they were quickly moved elsewhere.

Almost twenty years after the Paris Peace Accords, the political climate was changing. By 1991, The Soviet Union fell apart in separate countries, and the United States began to reestablish relations with Russia. The US also began to reach out to Vietnam, and one of the things they wanted answers about were the MIAs from the conflict. Rumors and reports continued to come out of Vietnam and Laos about American soldiers spotted in prisons or forced to work in labor camps.

The black POW-MIA flag became popular to commemorate those who were missing in action and possibly still held as prisoners of war. Image courtesy of zhukovsky via Deposit Photos.

A report from 1991 in Thailand claimed that a Thai citizen approached a US serviceman and gave him a list of four American POWs who had supposedly been sighted in Thailand near the Laos border. One of those names was Peter Cressman, one of the Baron 52 radio operators.

The US Senate created a committee to investigate the

MIA/POWs in 1991, and the back-end crew of Baron 52 were one of the groups they paid special attention to.

Finally able to enter Laos, US investigators returned to the site of the crash. Nothing soft like human bodies or fabric could survive in the jungle for that long. The searchers found some bone fragments and a tooth. A forensic expert reported that he could not verify that the bones were human. The tooth was supposed to belong to Peter Cressman, but when his family had the DNA tested, it was inconclusive, meaning they couldn't tell who it belonged to. The investigators also found one dog tag from one of the missing radio operators, Matejov. Testing on the dog tag to determine its age and authenticity was also inconclusive.

The US Department of Defense concluded, "The available biological evidence does not establish that all eight manifested crewman are represented in these remains."

The investigators also interviewed people from the local village. At this point, those who remembered the crash had been young when it happened, and they were recalling things that had occurred decades before. They said they reached the site before the search and rescue crews and didn't see any survivors. They described the scene somewhat differently than the search and rescue crew, saying one body was outside of the plane and that the search and rescue crew had set the plane on fire again when they left. It's hard to say if their memories were accurate after so long, but the body outside the plane is interesting, since the search and rescue crew only saw bodies in the plane. The Laos villagers wouldn't have touched the body because of their religious beliefs about not disturbing the dead, but an animal might have moved it. Or an enemy soldier or crash survivor could have.

In addition to the small bone fragments, the new search team also found many parts of the plane. They still didn't discover the jump door that would have allowed the men to parachute out or any sign of the electronic equipment that was top secret in the 1970s. At some point, that valuable equipment vanished. It might have burned along with the plane as the Laos villagers suggested. Perhaps it was seized by the North Vietnamese forces, who must have reached the plane—and any possible survivors—before the American recovery team.

The search team uncovered the zippers from the flight suits of five of the eight men (only the metal survived the hot and wet conditions). Most tellingly, they collected v-rings that were part of the parachutes. The v-rings show that eight parachutes were destroyed in the crash.

The plane had to have at least eight parachutes—one for each crewman—and could have had ten parachutes at the most. The number varied by plane and crew, if they carried any extra. We simply don't know if eight, nine, or ten parachutes were on the plane when Baron 52 took off. If anyone recorded that fact, the information is now lost. At worst, the recovered v-rings mean that none of the eight men parachuted out of the plane. But it leaves the possibility open that one or two parachuted out—or a very unlikely scenario where the four men in the back of the plane—the less damaged part—somehow survived the violent and fiery crash and were taken prisoner.

Because there's still the mystery of the four air pirates. If fewer than four men survived the crash, then we don't know who the air pirates were and what happened to them after that strange radio communication.

Just as the investigation was occurring, then-Russian-president Boris Yeltsin gave an interview distributed by the Associated Press about American prisoners of war from World War I, World War II, and Vietnam. Yeltsin acknowledged that some US citizens had been secretly held in Russia as POWs after each of those wars.

"Most of them have died," he said, but regarding the possibility that some were still alive in 1992, he admitted, "It is not excluded."

Meanwhile, the US Senate committee announced that they had received a list of aircraft downed along the Ho Chi Minh trail in Laos. Baron 52 was not on the list. Not only did North Vietnam claim not to have any prisoners from Baron 52—they claimed they had no record of encountering and shooting the plane.

Despite Yeltsin's comments, the unverified reports of American POW sightings, and the inconclusive bone fragments, the US Senate committee decided that all eight of those aboard Baron 52 had died in the accident. The radio report about the air pirates, they said, had been broadcast from North Vietnam and so had nothing to do with Baron 52. The fact that no one on the plane radioed for help meant that they crashed too quickly to have escaped from the plane. The Senate committee concluded that the US had not left any living POWs behind.

The military held a group burial for Baron 52's crew at Arlington National Cemetery in Washington D.C.

Most of the families of the missing men do not believe the government's conclusion. They refuse to accept the life insurance payout for the men's deaths or the inclusion of their names on the Vietnam Memorial that lists those killed in the conflict. They think the US government is hiding its mistakes in the Vietnam War. They want to hear the unedited and untranslated recordings of the reports of the four captured air pirates. They want some kind of proof of what the government claims. Mostly, they just want to know for certain what happened to their missing family members.

The Vietnam Memorial in Washington D.C. includes the names of those killed in the conflict. Image courtesy of the Historic American Buildings Survey, Library of Congress.

CHAPTER ELEVEN

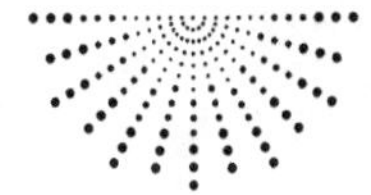

Will the real thief please raise Perón's hand?

In 1987, the government of Argentina received a ransom note demanding eight million US dollars for a kidnapping victim. Enemy forces sometimes hold citizens captive to demand money or changes from governments, but two things made this a very strange ransom case. The first was that the person in question was former Argentinian president Juan Perón, who had been dead since 1974. The second was that the thieves had only stolen one part of Perón: his hands.

The government refused to pay the ransom, which is common when dealing with kidnappers. Perón's hands remain missing to this day. The theft is shrouded in mystery and danger. We don't know who stole the hands, why they did it, or where the hands are now. Yet people who have investigated the missing hands have been threatened or killed in mysterious accidents, and rumors abound about mobsters and magic rituals involved with the hands.

Why would anyone care so much about the hands of a dead president?

Juan Perón on the right raises his hands in triumph. The thieves took his hands away, but we don't know why. Image courtesy of Wikimedia.

Juan Perón, along with his wife Evita, were among the most important figures in twentieth-century Argentina. Perón made huge changes to the country, which some loved and some hated. People in Argentina still argue about his ideas today. He is dead, but his legacy is alive.

Perón was born to a family of Argentinian sheep farmers and joined the military to have more options in life. Argentina had been a wealthy nation until the Great Depression collapsed the world's economy in 1929. While Perón studied military strategy in the 1930s, political groups argued over how to help Argentina's economy recover. Most people in Argentina believed their government was corrupt. They didn't trust the elections. Politicians accused each other of fraud and even hit and shot at one another.

In 1943, the Argentinian military decided to take over the government. Perón was given the job of Secretary of Labor, managing relationships with Argentina's workers. Most people considered it an unimportant job, but Perón took it seriously. He agreed to help the workers, and in exchange, they supported him and gave him more power.

While helping the poor of Argentina, he met actress and radio star Eva Duarte, known to her fans as Evita. Evita was like the Taylor Swift of her day—talented, popular, and a clever businesswoman. She had come from a poor background, and the common people loved her. Perón was already a favorite of the working class for supporting laws that benefited them. He and Evita became a power couple in Argentina, especially among the large population of workers.

By 1945, some Argentinian leaders didn't like Perón's growing influence. They had him removed from the government and arrested. Evita rallied the people in his defense. So many people showed up to protest that the government freed Perón.

Perón married Evita, and in 1946, he was elected president. Argentina had remained neutral in World Wars I and II, and Perón avoided involvement in the Cold War. He hoped to be able to trade with countries no matter what their policies, which he called the "Third Way." He allowed both Jewish refugees and Nazi war criminals to settle in Argentina and tried to stay friendly with the United States and the Soviet Union. He built factories and other projects to expand the economy and give Argentinians jobs.

Meanwhile, Evita established hospitals, schools, and

orphanages and organized Argentina's women to get the vote. She was possibly even more popular than her husband.

For a few years, Perón's policies worked. But his neutrality made it hard for any of his potential allies (especially the United States) to trust him, so he struggled with foreign relations. Droughts crippled Argentina's agriculture. Perón spent huge amounts of money for the government to take control of the railroads, banks, trade, and fuel, until the government ran out of funds. Then Evita died of cancer in 1952, taking away one of Perón's most important allies.

She was so beloved that Perón had her body preserved and put on display in a glass coffin, and people continued to visit her.

Perón and Evita were Argentina's power couple. Image courtesy of Wikimedia.

Some Argentinians, though, raised concerns about Perón's management and the country's huge amount of debt. In response, he shut down the newspapers and exiled anyone who questioned him. He encouraged his followers to attack those who opposed them. This led to increasing unease and violence in Argentina.

In 1955, the military led another revolt—this time against Perón. He fled to Europe.

When Perón escaped, the military stole Evita's body and sent it to Italy to be buried in secret. They hoped to erase all memories of Perón and his popularity. This started the history of body snatching around Perón that would end in the strange tale of his stolen hands.

But Evita was not forgotten. People in the capital city Buenos Aires drew graffiti asking, "Where is Eva Perón's body?"

Perón spent most of the remainder of his life in exile in Europe, where he remarried to fellow Argentinian Isabel Martinez. He remained popular with a large segment of Argentinians, and he worked from Europe to influence his followers. They advanced his policies of independence from other countries and government control of resources. He also made new allies in Europe—sometimes people with violent or criminal pasts, and even one who claimed to be a warlock with powerful magic.

One of Perón's followers became president of Argentina in 1973. He invited Perón to return to Argentina and take control of the government.

On regaining power, Perón delivered the ominous warning, "For our friends, everything. For our enemies, not even justice."

But Perón's health was failing, and he died the next year.

A group of Perón's supporters kidnapped and murdered the former military leader who had been responsible for stealing Evita's body. They then held the man's body for ransom until Evita's body was returned to Argentina.

Perón and Evita were buried—separately—in secure vaults.

Perón's new wife Isabel had been his vice president, so she became president of Argentina at his death. She was the first woman to be the president of a country (and only two countries had female prime ministers before this). She was not experienced with politics or popular with the military or the people. In 1976, they overthrew her government and drove her from the country. From that time until 1983, Argentina experienced the "Dirty War," where the military government frequently killed or "disappeared" anyone opposed to it.

Isabel Perón (center) became the world's first female president when her husband died, but she lacked Juan Perón's popularity and political skill. Image courtesy of Wikimedia.

Democracy was finally established again in Argentina in 1983, and some of the elected members of the government were followers of Perón. The tension between people who were for and against Perón continued to divide Argentina.

Then came the ransom note.

The note threatened to destroy Perón's hands if the kidnappers were not paid. The thieves claimed that Perón owed them the money before he died. They signed the ransom note, "Hermes IAI and the 13," a reference to Cuban revolutionaries who had died in the 1960s fighting the military government with Perón's supporters. The kidnapping note also quoted a poem from Isabel that she had left in the coffin with Perón—a note that presumably the thieves could only know about if they had broken into the grave. It referenced his hands, reading, *"Do you remember Juan, when holding hands, we walked through the garden, and you plucked a flower for me as proof of your love."*

Authorities rushed to the grave of Perón and found that, indeed, someone had broken into his crypt to cut off and steal his hands.

Perón's coffin was protected by iron bars, four locks that each required three keys to open, and a heavy glass lid weighing more than 300 pounds. The thieves had unlocked the coffin and the door to the crypt, though they broke the skylight and the glass lid and closed the locks to make it look as though they had forced their way in. There was supposed to only be one copy of the keys, and the government had them. People at the time assumed the thieves must have picked the locks. The thieves had carefully cut off Perón's hands and also stolen his military sword.

One man immediately claimed responsibility for the theft. Juan Alberto Imbesi was a former spy for the military government that had ousted Perón's party from power in 1955. He said that the hands had been smuggled out of South America to Spain. He also named five accomplices in the theft. Those five men had once been involved in a truck robbery, but the judge overseeing the case could find no connection between them and the conspiracy to steal Perón's hands. In fact, he questioned whether Imbesi was even involved, or if the former spy's mental health had failed and he was making his story up.

The authorities followed every lead they could find, but they recovered no trace of Perón's hands or his sword.

Despite this, the thieves weren't done covering their tracks.

Several people who worked at the cemetery came forward to say they'd seen something the night of the theft. They were each murdered, and their killers were never identified.

Kidnappers tried to grab the judge's wife, and she barely escaped.

A journalist and political activist reported that someone had broken into his home. He was afraid they had intended to leave Perón's hands in his house and frame him for the crime.

After a year of investigating the theft, the judge was killed in a car accident. Many found that suspicious, especially because the accident was so violent that his car flipped over and caught fire.

The next judge who took over the investigation quickly labeled the theft "unsolved" and closed the case.

Then in 1994, a second set of keys to the coffin were

discovered in a Buenos Aires police station. Only one set of keys was supposed to exist, so whoever had stolen the hands and the sword had somehow gained access to the original keys to copy them. Still, this new clue only added more mystery to the case. People came up with many theories about who stole Perón's hands.

Some people blamed the theft on Italian mob boss and secret society founder Licio Gelli. Gelli had supported Perón and therefore might view him as owing him a favor (or a lot of money). Gelli was a mafia member and a fascist allied with the Nazis during WWII. He had fled to Argentina after the war and built up an international network of political and financial connections, including Perón. Some people suspected him of being a spy or double agent for the US, especially because he was invited to US President Ronald Reagan's oath of office in 1981—an unusual offer for an Italian mob boss. Gelli denied knowing anything about Perón's hands, but he kept many secrets. When he died in 2015, a batch of his papers called the 500 Directory, with damaging information he kept about politicians, businessmen, and other leaders, vanished. Whatever secrets they held—possibly about Perón's hands—are still lost in the shadows.

Other people suggested that Perón's hands had been stolen to be used in a magic ritual. This might seem far-fetched, but Perón and Isabel and some of their followers believed in witchcraft and magic. One of their main advisors was a self-styled warlock who tried (and failed) to raise Perón from the dead.

Another line of thought is that the thieves wanted his

hands for his fingerprints, a ring he wore, or even his DNA. Some people have suggested his hands might be the key to opening a vault full of treasure in Switzerland—though fingerprint locks didn't exist in the 1970s when he died, so it seems unlikely.

One of Perón's many political enemies may have taken his hands as a symbol of taking away his power or control. Maybe an ally of the military leader who was murdered and then held for ransom to demand the return of Evita's body?

Or perhaps it was someone trying to destabilize the new democracy in Argentina. Not everyone likes to share power, and some may have hoped to sway the people or the government. There were huge protests when people heard about the thefts, with many of Perón's fans devastated by the news.

What about Cuba? The note referenced communist Cuban revolutionaries who died fighting in Argentina. Perón's neutral stance had made Argentina one of communist Cuba's few friends. Cuba as a nation had little to gain by upsetting Argentina, so the reference seems to have more to do with the fighting between factions in Argentina than with Cuba itself. Or perhaps the number 13 was significant, especially since the hands were stolen 13 years after Perón died.

Also, did including the poem in the ransom note have any special meaning beyond proving the thieves had been in the tomb? Maybe it was a message to Isabel Perón (who is still alive in 2024) or someone else?

In 2008, a new judge tried to get permission from the government to talk to people about top-secret matters related to the theft. He had a suspicion about who might have committed the theft, though not necessarily who hired the thieves. Before he could investigate further, someone broke into his house and stole all his files about the case as well as his laptop, making all his evidence vanish.

Whoever stole the hands was still out there and wanted the hands to stay lost.

The more time passes, the less likely we are to ever find an answer about Perón's hands, as witnesses die and evidence disappears.

CHAPTER TWELVE

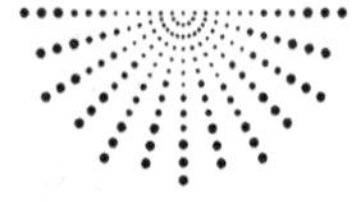

Tank Man

It is one of the most famous pictures of the twentieth century: a lone Chinese man, holding his sacks of groceries, stopped in the middle of the street to block a line of tanks towering over him. It was June 5, 1989, and China had just massacred hundreds of protesters at Tiananmen Square, where they were calling for more freedom. We don't know who the man was, why he was willing to risk death to defy the tanks, or what became of him. Often called Tank Man or the Lone Rebel, his image stirred the world.

China had been ruled by the communist party since 1949. The communists had promised solutions to the corruption and inequalities in China under the imperial dynasties and corrupt military government that followed. But flawed economic changes led tens of millions of people to starve, and ethnic minorities and religious groups faced persecution, oppression, imprisonment, and torture. Many Chinese people—especially young ones—hoped for change to bring more democracy and freedom of speech and religion to their country. When a communist leader who had promised more freedoms died, people gathered at Tiananmen Square in Beijing to mourn and then to protest the changes that didn't seem to be coming.

On June 4, 1989, China chose to end the peaceful protest by turning the military on the protesters, many of whom were students. Citizens of Beijing tried to stop the approaching tanks with barricades and even fighting, but the soldiers gunned down citizens who stood in their way, and the tanks rolled through to the square. They surrounded the protesters and fired without warning. As people fled the square, the soldiers shot them in the back. Medics who tried to help the injured were also killed. At the least, hundreds of people died, and it may have been as many as ten thousand.

A statue in Liberty Sculpture Park in Yermo, California commemorates Tank Man's stand against the tank. Image from ZUMA via Alamy.

It was the next day, when the tanks left down the Avenue of Eternal Peace, that Tank Man stood in their way. The tanks tried to go around, first one way, and then the other. But the man stepped into their path. He was carrying groceries home. He doesn't seem to have been one of the protesters in the square. He appears to have been an ordinary man who simply decided to make a stand, right in that time and place. He may have expected to die after so many others had, but he apparently decided at that moment he had to do something.

The tanks did not kill him. Maybe the soldiers were tired of killing, or maybe they admired his courage. Tank Man and the tanks stood facing each other for several silent, tense minutes. Then, Tank Man climbed up on the tank and spoke to the men inside. We don't know what they said to each other. Someone from the crowd—either onlookers or members of the military—grabbed Tank Man and hauled him away from the scene.

And from there he disappeared.

We don't know who he was. We don't know what happened to him after that moment.

The Chinese media and government never said anything about Tank Man. We only know about him because his stand occurred outside the Beijing Hotel, where foreign journalists were laying low during the protests. It was illegal for them to take pictures, but they found ways to sneak their cameras in and smuggle the film (necessary for taking pictures before digital cameras) out of the country.

One photographer, Charlie Cole, snapped his pictures and then hid the film in the toilet tank when Chinese authorities broke down his door and searched his hotel room.

Before digital cameras, photos were captured on film, which could easily be damaged or destroyed, erasing pictures forever. Image courtesy of Jakub T. Jankiewicz via Wikimedia license CC-BY-SA 4.0 International.

Jeff Widener, a photographer for the Associated Press, had been injured while taking pictures of the protest and was desperately ill with the flu, but he wanted a photo of the tanks. He was out of film for his camera but was able to get a roll from some tourists.

Time magazine reported on Widener's memories of Tank Man. "I assume he thinks he's going to die. But he doesn't care, because for whatever reason—either he's lost a loved one or he's just had it with the government, or whatever it is —his statement is more important than his own life."

In the days before instant pictures and internet uploads, Widener and the other journalists had to sneak their film out to safety. Widener made friends with an American foreign exchange student at the hotel, Kirk Martsen, who hid the film in his underwear to smuggle it out of the building. Martsen dodged soldiers and gunfire to hand the film off to the US Embassy, where it could be sent to the rest of the world.

The photos by Widener, Cole, and other journalists made

the front pages of newspapers around the globe. And they represent all the world knows of Tank Man.

Photos of Tank Man are used to remember the Tiananmen Square massacre, such as this one at a memorial service in Japan. Image from UPI via Alamy.

A British tabloid reporter claimed that Tank Man was a 19-year old son of factory workers named Wang Weilin, but no one has ever confirmed this or learned where the reporter got his information. Most doubt his claim since the reporter was never in China and tabloids are known for not checking facts carefully.

Many people are concerned that Tank Man was apprehended and killed by the Chinese government like hundreds of other protesters. It's possible. Thousands were arrested and at least some of them executed.

The Chinese government does not like to speak about Tiananmen Square and is usually silent about the "June 4th Incident" and Tank Man. But the *Los Angeles Times* reports on an interview with Chinese leader Jiang Zemin ten years after the incident. When asked about Tank Man, Jiang said the government hunted for him but never found him.

"I think never killed," Jiang said.

We can hope that's true, but the Chinese government has been secretive about some of its activities, so we can't be certain.

After the massacre, an unlikely alliance formed to help the protest organizers who had survived. Based in Hong Kong, which at the time was free from Chinese control, it was called Operation Yellowbird. A variety of people interested in democracy or free trade in China, ranging from the US CIA to Hong Kong business leaders to the Chinese mob, helped to smuggle some Tiananmen Square protesters into Hong Kong. They wore disguises, hid out in factories, communicated with secret codes, and eventually were smuggled out of the country by boat.

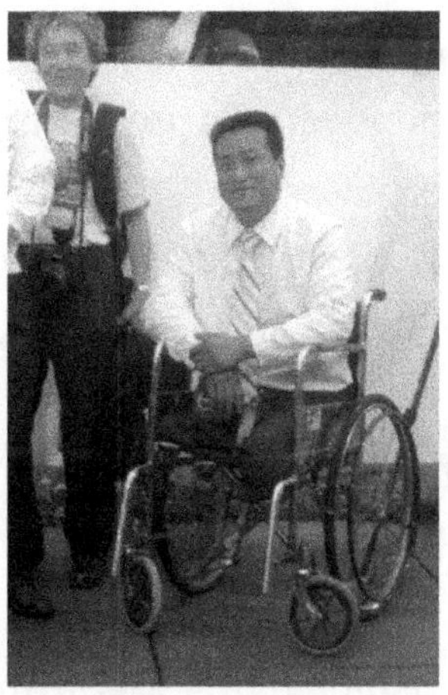

Fang Zheng's legs were crushed by a tank during the Tiananmen Square protests. He became a para athlete and escaped China to work for freedom for his home country. Image courtesy of Prince Roy via Flickr license CC-BY-2.0 DEED.

From Hong Kong, most escapees went to France and the

United States. Some of the protesters found their own way to Hong Kong and were likewise able to escape from China.

Could Tank Man have fled as well? Maybe.

No one has ever come forward with a viable claim to being Tank Man. It seems like someone who escaped from China and was famous for his role in the protests would make a claim to his identity. But there could be a good reason he has remained silent—if he did escape. Even many years after escaping China, the known protesters who resettled in other countries are still under surveillance by China. One escaped protester, Yan Xiong, served in the US military as a chaplain and later tried to run for US Congress. But then he noticed people following him in cars and trying to stop him from speaking. The FBI warned him that China had hired people to stop him from running for political office—by spreading rumors about him, intimidating him, even beating him or killing him if necessary. China couldn't recapture the escaped protesters, but it was still watching them and trying to sabotage their lives—especially if they wanted a position of influence.

So, if Tank Man did escape China, he may have very wisely decided to keep his role a secret. If China doesn't know who he is, he would want to keep it that way.

Tank Man may also be living an ordinary life in China. In fact, if he's still in China, he probably doesn't know he's famous. The pictures taken of him were never published in China—they are banned there, as is most talk of the "June 4th Incident." Many younger Chinese people don't know much if anything about what happened at Tiananmen Square in 1989. Tank Man may be living with a secret memory of the time he stood up to the tanks, unaware that many consider him a hero. He might fear to ever speak of his act of defiance.

But the secret isn't completely buried. The number "64" is forbidden for many uses in China since it's the date of the massacre (6-4). And some people in China and Chinese-influenced regions like Hong Kong and Taiwan still use the number as a code for what happened that day. Some outside China even celebrate a remembrance day on June 4th. They want to make certain that China cannot erase the memory of what it did in Tiananmen Square, and that the people of China can still hope for freedom.

In the meantime, Tank Man has become an image of bravery, of peaceful protest, and of the power of one against great forces. Whether he died in 1989, is living a new life in secret, or is unaware of the impact he had, his moment of defiance provided inspiration and hope to many that human dignity can still win against the darker forces in the world.

Graffiti of Tank Man is used to rally people for greater freedom. Image courtesy of Disappearing Act via Flickr license CC-BY-SA 2.0 DEED.

CHAPTER THIRTEEN

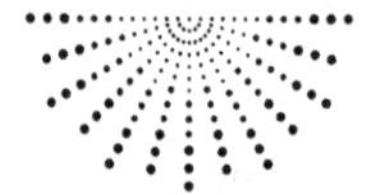

Unidentified Flying Objects

The sight shocked the people of San Francisco: a strange light moved through the night. It seemed to be attached to an airship shaped like a hotdog. Some said they even heard voices from the ship.

KQED quoted several witnesses describing it. "[The airship] was high in the heavens and appeared to be of huge size... It moved rapidly, going at least twenty miles per hour. It shot across the skies in the northwest, then turned quickly and disappeared..." Another added, "The light was far brighter than any of the electric lights I saw just below..."

The *San Fransisco Call and Post* added another account from a witness who was driving when the ship passed over him. His passengers demanded he stop so they could get a better look. “They got out in the road and looked up at the airship, the most surprised crowd I ever saw in my life. There it was, sure enough, right overhead and traveling on at a good rate, with its light blazing away, and the most uncanny-looking thing I ever saw. Airship or anything else, it was the most remarkable-looking object, and I am at a loss now to convince myself that I actually saw it.”

Later sightings occurred in other parts of the United States. This included unverified reports of an attempted abduction and a crash that supposedly left behind an inhuman corpse.

Kansas! magazine reported that a farmer said he, “saw to my utter amazement an airship slowly descending over my cow lot...” One cow started making a racket, and he claimed that a thick cable from the airship had snagged her. “We tried to get it off but could not, so we cut the wire loose and stood in amazement to see ship, cow, and all rise slowly and sail off, disappearing in the northwest.”

Some people thought the witnesses had been drunk or trying to pull a hoax. Many believed they were glimpsing secret tests of a new technology. Others were certain invaders from another planet had reached Earth.

Sound familiar? Unidentified Flying Object or UFO sightings are as much a part of the modern world as cars and computers. What sets this “UFO panic” apart is that it took place in 1896 and 1897. It was the first UFO craze of the modern world—but it wouldn’t be the last.

A drawing of the airship people described seeing in 1896 and 1897. It resembles a zeppelin, which had been invented in Europe but not yet reached the United States. Image courtesy of Library of Congress Chronicling America.

In 1947, US pilot Kenneth Arnold in Washington, United States, reported nine glowing blue objects speeding past him in a V-formation. According to the National Air and Space Museum, he said, "It startled me. I just assumed it was some military lieutenant out with a shiny P-51 and I had [caught] the reflection of the sun hitting the wings of his plane." Then he realized these moved like no aircraft that he knew. He guessed their speed to be 1,700 miles per hour (modern passenger jets go about 900 mph). He said they moved like a saucer skipping across water, leading to the term "flying saucer."

Arnold's story spread, and over the next few weeks, other people in the United States also reported seeing "flying saucers."

This culminated with the Roswell Incident in Roswell, New Mexico. A rancher near Roswell found pieces of metal, plastic, and paper in one of his fields. With flying saucers on everyone's mind, the public became convinced that a flying saucer had crashed in New Mexico, and the modern alien craze began.

Some of the debris from the Roswell Incident. Image courtesy of the Fort Worth Star-Telegram Photograph Collection, Special Collections, The University of Texas at Arlington Library, Arlington, Texas license CC-BY 4.0.

Government officials at the time said the crashed object was a weather balloon. Later declassified papers say the weather balloon claim is partly true. It was actually a spy balloon being used to check the atmosphere for signs that Russia was testing nuclear weapons.

This was just following World War II, and the Cold War between the United States and the Soviet Union had begun. Both countries had nuclear weapons, so a "hot war" involving direct fighting would have devastated the world, poisoning the water and air with radiation. Instead, both countries competed in other ways, especially in developing new technologies. Spying and secrets were a major part of the Cold War.

The US government later admitted responsibility and a cover-up of the Roswell incident, but they can't explain Arnold's sighting. Was it an experiment by Russia or another country? The government wanted to know, so the Air Force started a secret program called Project Blue Book to study UFOs from 1952 to 1969.

In 1955, the government also acquired a remote testing site in Nevada near Groom Dry Lake. Though the site is sometimes called Groom Lake, Dreamland, or Paradise Ranch, most people know it best as Area 51.

Area 51 is near the Nevada Test Site where the government conducted early nuclear testing. It's also where several spy planes were developed and tested. These planes could fly higher and faster than regular aircraft and often had strange shapes to avoid detection by radar. Project Blue Book concluded that many UFO sightings from the 1950s and 60s could be traced to spy planes. Of course, they didn't confess this to the public for many years.

An image from Project Blue Book showing a 1952 UFO sighting, made public without an explanation for the lights. Image courtesy of the Library of Congress.

The government did not admit the existence of Area 51 until 2013, but the location has long been part of UFO lore. The site is still top secret, and many wonder if the government is holding more technology there—perhaps related to extraterrestrials.

Radar testing on an airplane design at Area 51. Image courtesy of the US CIA.

Many UFOs sightings occur in the western United States, which could support the theory that they're related to government tests of secret technology. In 1951, residents of Lubbock, Texas saw lights flying by in the evening sky. The stereotype is that UFO sightings are experienced by eccentric people living out in the middle of nowhere, but these were college professors and students. Then, in 1957, another sighting of strange lights in Texas was accompanying by cars and other electronics suddenly not working. And in eastern Utah in the 1960s and 1970s, many residents commonly saw strange lights and aircraft in the sky.

In fact, eastern Utah continues to be a hotbed of UFO sightings.

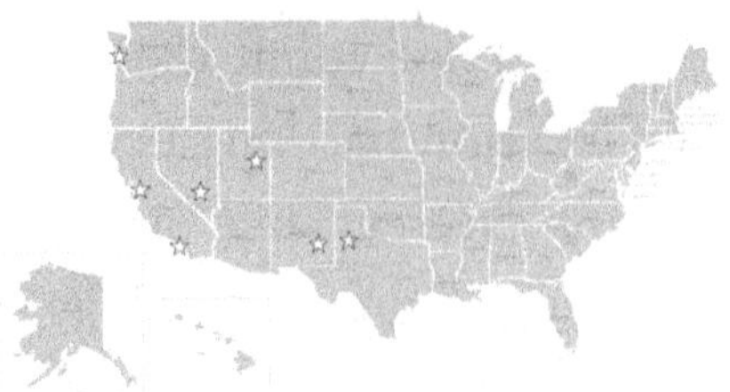

Some important UFO sites in the Western United States. Original map by pyty via Deposit Photos (modified).

Project Blue Book shut down in 1969, viewed by many politicians and scientists as a waste of time and money. The US government continued to publicly disavow any unexplained paranormal activity, but they were quietly interested, and eastern Utah caught their attention.

The most famous site for paranormal or extraterrestrial activity in eastern Utah is the place now known as Skinwalker Ranch. The ranch, more properly named Sherman Ranch (the term Skinwalker was taken from Navajo beliefs about evil and dangerous beings), is near the Ute reservation and the small town of Vernal, Utah. The ranch was homesteaded by the Myers family for 60 years, during which time they reported nothing strange. But in the 1990s, the Myers sold the ranch to the Shermans. The Shermans lived on the ranch for two years, and they reported numerous problems with the property, such as cattle found dead with their tongues removed, strange lights in the sky, and magnetic and electronic malfunctions.

The Shermans were happy to sell the ranch and move to another one a little farther away.

Terry Sherman told the Las Vegas Sun, “It's just been a

bad deal all the way around. All that's really redeeming is that you have some knowledge that a lot of people don't have, for what it's worth."

The person willing to buy their "haunted" property was wealthy paranormal investigator Robert Bigelow. Bigelow's interest in the ranch wasn't odd. He founded the National Institute for Discovery Science (NIDS) to investigate unexplained phenomena. The thing that is odd is that the US government joined him in his investigations on the ranch—and they kept everything they studied secret.

The government wasn't ready to declare that UFOs were real, but they were willing to investigate again. So, military personnel joined Bigelow at Sherman Ranch along with veterinarians and scientists. Bigelow's investigations lasted for twenty years, ending in 2016 when he sold the ranch to Utah real estate millionaire Brandon Fugal. The government has no comment on the results of their research there. Did they find something dangerous? Or are they just embarrassed that they spent millions of taxpayer dollars on a dead end?

One researcher on the case told reporter George Knapp, "We probably have, if you count all the pre-NIDS and post-NIDS incidents, close to 100 different incidents."

Yet we don't have access to the reports of those "incidents."

Under Fugal's ownership, the ranch has been featured on paranormal investigation TV shows, but they don't offer any solid proof of what caused the strange events at the ranch.

The US government hasn't revealed what they learned at

Sherman Ranch, but the public does know about the *Nimitz* sighting.

The *USS Nimitz* is a US aircraft carrier. In 2004, its radars picked up “anomalies,” and it sent planes out to investigate. The military pilots reported objects shaped like tic-tac candies zipping around the ocean, moving in ways that no current aircraft can move and at high speeds. The military even captured recordings of the UFOs’ actions.

One of the pilots later told the US Congress, "The technology that we faced is far superior to anything that we had, and there’s nothing we can do about it, nothing” (as reported by NBC News).

All of these examples are in the United States, but if aliens are visiting our modern world, they’re not limiting themselves to the USA.

UFO “hotspots” around the world.

In October of 1954, a football (soccer) game in Florence, Italy ground to a halt. Fans and players alike forgot the game because an egg-shaped UFO hovered over the stadium. People all across Italy reported the phenomenon over the next few days. The UFOs dropped a fine, white stringy substance below them. It disintegrated quickly, but one scientist was able to analyze a small sample and found that it wasn't radioactive and contained elements found on Earth like boron, magnesium, and silicon. Some skeptics said the people were witnessing a massive migration of spiders that spin webs to parachute across the sky, but spider silk usually doesn't contain boron or silicon.

In Melbourne, Australia in 1966, a group of students and teachers at Westfall School watched a saucer-shaped aircraft circle their school several times.

In the 1970s, an Iranian pilot encountered a strange light in the sky, and his instruments failed. An investigation involving both the Iranian and US military failed to identify the light. In fact, along with the Western US and Japan (especially the nuclear bomb sites of Nagasaki and Hiroshima), this region of the Middle East is considered a UFO hotspot.

A plane in New Zealand flying over the Kaikōura Mountain Range in 1978 noticed lights and an unidentified flying object tracking their plane. The radar on the ground at Wellington, the capital city, also captured the unidentified craft. An Australian television crew reporting on the incident caught a reappearance of the phenomenon and even recorded the unknown object flying alongside their plane. Despite the number of witnesses and the recordings, no one has offered a satisfactory explanation for the Kaikōura lights.

Members of the US and British military saw strange lights above Rendlesham Forest in 1980 and found damaged trees and high levels of radiation when they went to investigate.

The UFOs apparently enjoyed the Italian football game and returned in 1982 over a football stadium in Brazil in front of thousands of people. And then on May 19, 1986, the UFOs returned to Brazil, with sightings and radar recordings across much of the country. When the reports of the incident were declassified in 2009, it confirmed that the Brazilian government had no explanation for the events, but that the objects could fly extremely fast, make sudden turns, and fly in formation.

At the end of 1989 and the beginning of 1990, people on the ground in Belgium reported seeing a strange object in the sky. Local pilots also encountered something in the sky moving very fast that they could see with their radar but not with their physical eyes. The Belgian air force then recorded a triangle-shaped craft with lights on each corner.

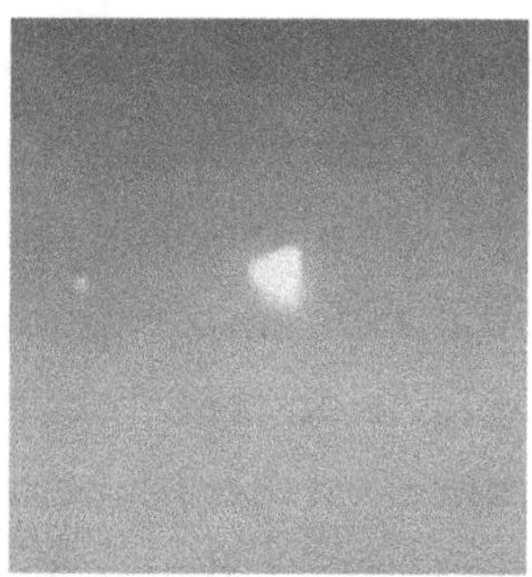

A still shot from a video taken by the US military of a triangle-shaped UFO in 2019. Image courtesy of Wikimedia.

Over 60 Zimbabwe school children in 1994 claimed a UFO landed by their school while they were outside and the teachers were in the building having a meeting. They recall that creatures in black clothing emerged from the craft, and some said the creatures warned them that danger was coming if they did not take better care of the environment. Other people in the region saw strange lights and a craft in the sky at the time.

These are only some of the UFO sightings that have occurred around the world in the last century—sightings which were witnessed by many people.

In 2017, a whistleblower uncovered the fact that the US government had been investigating UFOs once again. This led the US Congress to create a committee to investigate Unidentified Aerial Phenomenon or UAPs in 2023 and reveal their findings to the public.

NBC News quoted Representative Robert Garcia of the committee saying, "The sheer number of reports, whistleblowers and stories of unidentified anomalous phenomena should raise real questions and warrant investigation and oversight. And that's why we are here today. UAPs, whatever they may be, may pose a serious threat to our military or civilian aircraft. And that must be understood."

The committee heard testimony about secret government investigations, rumors of "nonhuman" biology, and many UFO sightings by military and commercial pilots. None of the evidence proved that aliens have visited Earth, but it also couldn't rule it out.

The committee's conclusion? Sometimes strange things happen, and we can't explain them.

So, it's still up to you to decide: Are aliens from another

planet or dimension visiting Earth? Or is someone on Earth developing advanced technologies that the rest of us are only glimpsing? Are we seeing things we can't explain and blaming aliens because we can't imagine we're alone in the vast expanse of space? Or does the universe still hold mysteries waiting for us to discover?

EPILOGUE: HOW A MODERN MYSTERY WAS SOLVED—SORT OF

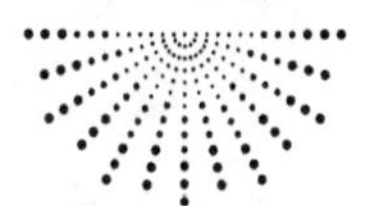

In 1948, beachgoers in Adelaide, Australia stumbled across a man in a suit lying on the sand. He appeared peaceful, though they found it strange that he wasn't moving. He was actually dead—and everything about him was a mystery.

Medical examiners couldn't determine his cause of death, but they suspected an unknown poison. He seemed to have died peacefully and without any signs of pain or struggle—which would be unusual for poison—so they suspected he might have died elsewhere and been moved to the beach. Yet some locals believed they saw him sitting on the beach the night before, still alive but moving slowly and strangely.

The police also couldn't determine who the man was. He was White, middle-aged, and in top athletic physical condition. His dental records didn't match any known person, and he didn't have a wallet or other identification, carrying only some cigarettes and matches, some chewing gum, a comb from the United States, a bus ticket, and an unused train ticket to leave Adelaide. His suit—which appeared to be made in the United States—had all the labels cut out. Investigators called him Somerton Man because he was found at Somerton Park Beach.

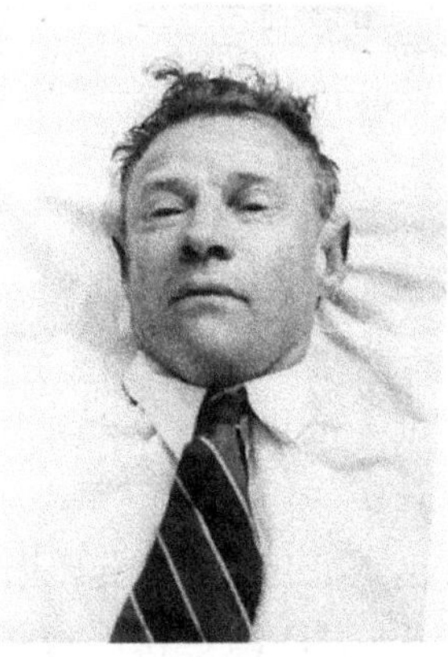

No one could identify the Somerton Man, though this picture of him was sent out all over Australia and the world. Image courtesy of the Australian government and Wikimedia.

The next break in the case came when the Adelaide Railway Station staff discovered an unclaimed suitcase. Inside, police found an unusual orange thread that exactly matched the thread that had been used to repair a hole in Somerton Man's pocket. There were few other clues in the suitcase. Most of the labels had been cut from the clothes again, but a couple of the items were labeled "T. Keane." A search in Australia, the United States, Britain, and other English-speaking countries around the world turned up no missing persons named T. Keane.

Investigators looked more closely at Somerton Man's

belongings. In the small front pocket of the trousers he wore when he died, they found a tiny, rolled up piece of paper that appeared to have been torn from a book. It read "*Tamám Shud,*" which is Persian for, "It is finished." The man appeared to be of White European ancestry, which made it more unusual that he would know Persian.

Police instituted a search for the book that could have produced the phrase. Someone in Adelaide came forward with a match: a translation of medieval Persian poems called *Rubaiyat of Omar Khayyám*. Though the last line was the Persian *Tamám Shud,* the book was translated to English, and its poems and message of finding pleasure in life had been popular before World War II. The unidentified man who discovered the book said he found it tossed into the back of a car. Part of the book's last page was torn: a perfect match for Somerton Man's scrap of paper.

The book contained a series of letters that looked like a code—a code which no one has ever been able to crack. It also had the phone number of a woman named Jessica "Jo" Thomson—who lived in Adelaide only about one city block from where Somerton Man was found.

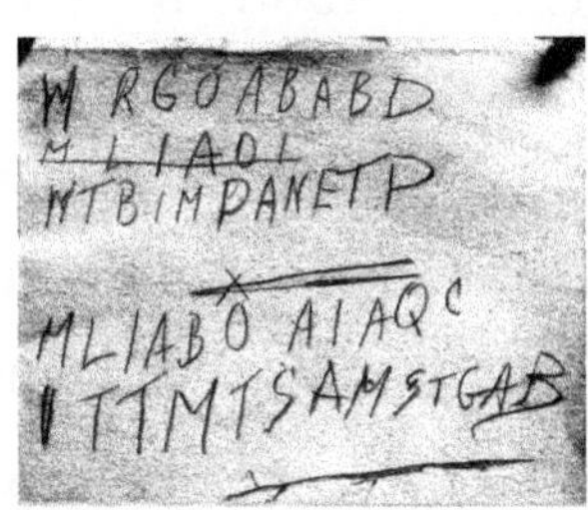

The code found in the book. Image courtesy of the Australian government and Wikimedia.

Thomson denied knowing anything about Somerton Man, though when shown a plaster cast of his face, she almost fainted. She said a strange man had been asking questions about her, but claimed to not know who he was. She had owned a copy of the *Rubaiyat* but gave it to a man she met while serving as a nurse during World War II. Police tracked down the man and found he still had the book with its final page and "*Tamám Shud*" intact.

Thomson had been a nurse, so she might know something about poisons, and many who knew her thought she was keeping a secret about Somerton Man. With Thomson's silence, however, Somerton Man's case went cold. Many people attempted to crack his code, and most people assumed he was a foreign spy killed at the start of the Cold War.

Only recently has anything changed, and that change is the result of family DNA now being used in criminal investigations. This technique involves taking the DNA of an unknown person—often one who committed a crime and left DNA behind—and comparing it to the DNA of known people who voluntarily submitted their DNA samples to public databases. This method of investigation has only become possible recently because many people have submitted their DNA for testing. Most people use DNA databases to learn more about their family's history and origins, or perhaps their medical conditions. Some of these databases are public, however, and police can use the DNA in those to find distant relatives of unknown people.

For instance, a mystery person might have a cousin who added their DNA to a public database. First cousins (people whose parents were siblings and share one set of common grandparents) have about 12.5% of their DNA in common through those grandparents. So, if a section of the mystery person's DNA matches 12.5% of a known person's DNA, investigators can guess that the mystery person is a cousin of the known person. Because DNA can also reveal things like biological sex and probable skin, eye, and hair color, it becomes much easier to narrow down who the mystery person is.

This is the case with Somerton Man. When the police made the cast of his face in 1949, some of his hair stuck to the plaster—and hair contains DNA that current researchers can study. In 2022, family DNA research narrowed down his likely identity to one set of siblings from Australia. It was simple to research the family and learn that of the three brothers from this family, one had died in World War II and one had lived past 1948—but one brother had gone missing in 1947. His name was Carl Webb.

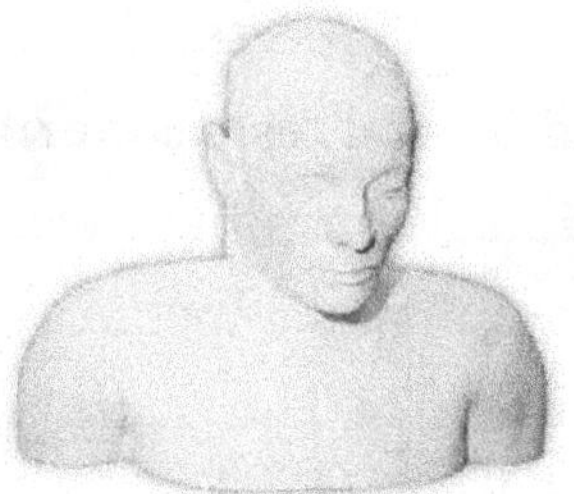

This plaster cast of the Somerton Man provided DNA that helped identify him. Image courtesy of the Australian government and Wikimedia.

Carl Webb had been an electrical engineer from Melbourne, Australia. He helped with his family's bakery and married in 1941 at the age of 36. His marriage was unhappy, and the couple eventually split up, with her moving far across the country to Adelaide. The last time she —or anyone—saw him was in early 1947 (his wife, apparently with no idea he was the dead mystery man, officially divorced him in 1951). Webb's sister was married to a Keane, which matches the last name found in the suitcase (some think the "T" was actually a "J" and the clothes had belonged to Webb's nephew John Keane, who served overseas and died in the war—clothes were often passed along and reused due to wartime shortages). Webb had enjoyed poetry and betting on horse races. Some think this means the code in the Persian poetry book was a system to keep track of race horses.

The Australian government is still conducting its own tests to verify Somerton Man's identity, but many consider the case closed through family DNA testing. It paints a picture of Carl Webb as a forgotten man dying alone on a beach.

But some think that Somerton Man has more mysteries to reveal—assuming official tests confirm his identity as Carl Webb. After all, medical examiners were convinced he was poisoned, and by an unusual substance that was difficult to trace. And what did Jessica Thomson know that she wasn't telling? If, "It is finished" was his final message, who was that message for and what was finished? As an engineer, Carl Webb could have lived a double life—perhaps as a spy. He must have been doing something in the year and a half between when his wife last saw him and when he turned up dead on the beach.

Smithsonian magazine quoted one of Somerton Man's researchers saying, "Some answers may come soon, some may take years, and some may never be answered." This applies not just to Somerton Man, but to all the mysteries of our modern world.

SELECTED SOURCES AND FURTHER READING

Disclaimer: The author and publisher provide these links for informational purposes only and do not endorse or control the content of any resources listed below. Hyperlinks may become out of date and some sources may contain ads or information that is inaccurate, outdated, or sensitive. The author and publisher assume no responsibility or liability for the content of outside sources.

Titanic Mystery Ship

Encyclopedia Titanica, https://www.encyclopedia-titanica.org/

Samuel Halpern, "The Almerian and the Mount Temple – A Tale of Two Ships," March 20, 2013, accessed at https://www.titanicology.com/Californian/The_Almerian_and_the_Mount_Temple.pdf

Charles Herbert Lightoller, "I Was There—The Sinking of the Titanic," BBC, 1936, accessed at https://www.titanicofficers.com/article_13.html

Charles Herbert Lightoller, Joseph Boxhall, et al, Testimony before the United States Senate Inquiry, accessed at https://www.titanicinquiry.org/index.php

Lieutenant Commander Craig McLean, NOAA, and David L. Eno, "The Case for Captain Lord," Naval History, Volume 6 Number 1, March 1992, accessed at https://www.usni.org/magazines/naval-history-magazine/1992/march/case-captain-lord

Emma Reynolds, news.com.au, "'His blood ran cold': Call that sealed fate of Titanic victims," accessed at https://www.news.com.au/lifestyle/real-life/true-stories/his-blood-ran-cold-call-that-sealed-fate-of-titanic-victims/news-story/9e292cc59fb35c3767370b8da6648f8e

Smithsonian Magazine, "Did the Titanic Sink Because of an Optical Illusion?" March 1, 2012, https://www.smithsonianmag.com/science-nature/did-the-titanic-sink-because-of-an-optical-illusion-102040309/

Titanic Belfast, "Finding Titanic: From Search to Seabed," accessed at https://www.titanicbelfast.com/history-of-titanic/titanic-stories/finding-titanic-from-search-to-seabed/

Who killed John Parr?

BBC News, "Daily Mirror Headlines: The Declaration of War, Published 4 August 1914, https://www.bbc.co.uk/history/worldwars/wwone/mirror01_01.shtml

Sean Clare, "WWI mystery: Who killed Private John Parr?" BBC News, August 4, 2014, accessed at https://www.bbc.com/news/uk-28442670

Imperial War Museums, "Voices of the First World War: Into Battle," accessed at https://www.iwm.org.uk/history/voices-of-the-first-world-war-into-battle

Our War, "Private John Henry Parr—An Investigation of the Evidence Behind His Story," May 2, 2021 https://ourwar1915.wordpress.com/2021/05/06/private-john-henry-parr-an-investigation-of-the-evidence-behind-his-story/

The Tsar's Lost Treasures

Claude Anet, Through the Russian revolution : notes of an eyewitness, from 12th March-30th May, 1917, Available at Internet Archive, https://archive.org/details/throughrussianre00anetiala/page/n9/mode/2up

Sarah Cascone, "U.S. Authorities May Have Found a Fabergé Egg Sitting Around on a Russian Oligarch's Seized $300 Million Yacht," artnet, July 22, 2022, accessed at https://news.artnet.com/art-world-archives/us-authorities-seize-faberge-egg-oligarchs-yacht-2150922#:~:text=One%20lost%20Imperial%20Egg%20did,it%20as%20a%20Faberg%C3%A9%20original.

Sarah Kuta, "'Alleged' Faberge Egg Found Aboard a Seized Russian Oligarch's Yacht," Smithsonian Magazine, July 26, 2022, accessed at https://www.smithsonianmag.com/smart-news/rare-faberge-egg-seized-russian-oligarch-yacht-180980471/

Emilie Le Beau Lucchesi, "How Scientists Identified the Remains of the Romanovs," Discover Magazine, April 15, 2022, accessed at https://www.discovermagazine.com/the-sciences/how-scientists-identified-the-remains-of-the-romanovs

Riteshdesai, "What happened to the Lost Treasure Of The Tsars," Medium, August 13, 2020, accessed at https://medium.com/@riteshdesai10001/what-happened-to-the-lost-treasure-of-the-tsars-76dd20e6fabc

Lina Zeldovich, "In search of Russia's lost gold," BBC Travel, October 23,

2017, accessed at https://www.bbc.com/travel/article/20171022-in-search-of-russias-lost-gold

Olivia Hosken, "The Enduring Mystery of the Romanovs' Missing Faberge Easter Eggs," *Town & Country*, April 5, 2020, accessed at https://www.townandcountrymag.com/style/jewelry-and-watches/a31991995/romanov-faberge-easter-eggs/

Deadly Beauty Sleep

Leslie Hoffman and Joel A. Vilensky, "Encephalitis lethargica: 100 years after the epidemic," *Brain*, Volume 140, Issue 8, August 2017, Pages 2246–2251, accessed at https://doi.org/10.1093/brain/awx177

John M. Barry, "The site of origin of the 1918 influenza pandemic and its public health implications," Journal of Translation Medicine, 2004, https://www.ncbi.nlm.nih.gov/pmc/articles/PMC340389/

Heidi Moawad, "Encephalitis Lethargica: The Still Unexplained Sleeping Sickness," NeurologyLive, February 12, 2018, accessed at https://www.neurologylive.com/view/encephalitis-lethargica-still-unexplained-sleeping-sickness

Christof Kock, "What a Long-Ago Epidemic Teaches Us about Sleep," Scientific American, March 1, 2016, accessed at https://www.scientificamerican.com/article/what-a-long-ago-epidemic-teaches-us-about-sleep/

Meilan Solly, "What We Can Learn From 1918 Influenza Diaries," Smithsonian Magazine, April 13, 2020, https://www.smithsonianmag.com/history/what-we-can-learn-1918-influenza-diaries-180974614/

Oliver Sacks, Awakenings, reprint edition, Vintage Press, October 5, 1999

The Lancet, April 20, 1918, accessed at https://www.thelancet.com/journals/lancet/issue/vol191no4938/PIIS0140-6736(00)X8248-7

The Indianapolis Times, "Sleep Disease Robs Victims of Moral Sense," July 31, 1925, available through the Library of Congress, Chronicling America, https://chroniclingamerica.loc.gov/lccn/sn82015313/1925-07-31/ed-1/seq-19/#date1=1916&sort=relevance&rows=20&words=sickness+Sleepy&searchType=basic&sequence=0&index=1&state=&date2=1930&proxtext=%22sleepy+sickness%22&y=15&x=19&dateFilterType=yearRange&page=3

Yorkville Enquirer, "Epidemic Diseases," March 29, 1921, available through the Library of Congress, Chronicling America, https://chroniclingamerica.loc.gov/lccn/sn84026925/1921-03-29/ed-1/seq-8/#date1=1916&sort=relevance&rows=20&words=sickness+sleepy&searchType=basic&sequence=0&index=6&state=&date2=1930&proxtext=%22sleepy+sickness%22&y=15&x=19&dateFilterType=yearRange&page=3

The Mummy's Curse

Bruce Bower, "King Tut's tomb still has secrets to reveal 100 years after its discovery," ScienceNews, November 2, 2022, accessed at https://www.sciencenews.org/article/king-tut-tutankhamun-tomb-discovery-archaeology

Sherif El-Tawil, "Lord Carnarvon's death: the curse of aspergillosis?" The Lancet, September 6, 2003, accessed at https://www.thelancet.com/journals/lancet/article/PIIS0140-6736(03)14268-7/fulltext

Jo Marchant, "How Howard Carter Discovered King Tut's Golden Tomb," Smithsonian Magazine, November 3, 2022, accessed at https://www.smithsonianmag.com/history/how-howard-carter-discovered-king-tuts-golden-tomb-180981052/

Jo Marchant, "The mummy's curse," aeon, accessed at https://aeon.co/essays/why-does-the-mummy-s-curse-refuse-to-die

Dr. Howard Markel, "Unlocking the medical mysteries of King Tut's tomb," PBS News, November 4, 2016, accessed at https://www.pbs.org/newshour/health/discovery-king-tuts-tomb

Paul Peachy, "The forgotten Egyptians who helped find Tutankhamun," The National News, April 15, 2022, accessed at https://www.thenationalnews.com/weekend/2022/04/15/the-forgotten-egyptians-who-helped-to-find-tutankhamun/

The Vanished Pilot

Larry Clark, "Still searching for Amelia," Washington State Magazine, August 2, 2018, accessed at https://news.wsu.edu/news/2018/08/02/still-searching-for-amelia/

Amelia Earhart, Last Flight, Crown Press, December 15, 2009.

Amelia Earhart, The Fun of It, Brewer Warren & Putnam, June 1, 1932

Amelia Earhart, 20 hours 40 minutes: Our Flight in the Friendship, Ayer Co Pub, December 1, 1979.

Megan Friedman, "A New Study May Have Identified Amelia Earhart's

Bones," Popular Mechanics, March 7, 2018, accessed at https://www.popularmechanics.com/science/a19170111/amelia-earhart-nikumamoro-island-bones-study/

Elizabeth Hanes, "Tantalizing Theories About the Earhart Disappearance," History, July 2, 2012, accessed at https://www.history.com/news/what-happened-to-amelia-9-tantalizing-theories-about-the-earhart-disappearance

Elizabeth Hanes, "Amelia Earhart's Navigator: The Life and Loss of Fred Noonan," History, May 20, 2024, accessed at https://www.history.com/news/amelia-earharts-navigator-the-life-and-loss-of-fred-noonan

James Pollard and Ben Finley, "Has Amelia Earhart's vanished plane finally been found?" PBS News, January 31, 2024, accessed at https://www.pbs.org/newshour/nation/has-amelia-earharts-vanished-plane-finally-been-found

John P. Riley Jr., "The Earhart Tragedy: Old Mystery, New Hypothesis," Naval History, Volume 14 Number 4, August 2000, accessed at https://www.usni.org/magazines/naval-history-magazine/2000/august/earhart-tragedy-old-mystery-new-hypothesis

TIGHAR, "Last Words," Earhart Project Research Bulletin, April 7, 2007, accessed at https://tighar.org/Projects/Earhart/Archives/Research/Bulletins/49_LastWords/49_LastWords.html

Ashley J. WennersHerron, "Investigating Amelia Earhart's disappearance mystery with neutrons," PennState Research News, January 28, 2021, accessed at https://www.psu.edu/news/research/story/investigating-amelia-earharts-disappearance-mystery-neutrons/

Lost Nazi Plunder

Jess Blumberg, "A Brief History of the Amber Room," Smithsonian Magazine, July 31, 2007, accessed at https://www.smithsonianmag.com/history/a-brief-history-of-the-amber-room-160940121/

Robert M Edsel, *Monuments Men*, Little, Brown & Company, October 22, 2013

Jake Halpern, "The Nazi Underground," The New Yorker, May 2, 2026, accessed at https://www.newyorker.com/magazine/2016/05/09/searching-for-nazi-gold

Mark Milligan, "What happened to the Nazi gold train?" February 16, 2024, accessed at https://www.heritagedaily.com/2024/02/what-happened-to-the-nazi-gold-train/150569

Jim Morrison, "The True Story of the Monuments Men," Smithsonian Magazine, February 7, 2014, accessed at https://www.smithsonianmag.com/history/true-story-monuments-men-180949569/#:~:text=In%20a%20race%20against%20time,years%20of%20culture%20by%20Nazis.

James Moske, "Stolen Treasure: Art and Archives at Neuschwanstein Castle," The Metropolitan Museum of Art, June 3, 2019, accessed at https://www.metmuseum.org/articles/provenance-research-james-rorimer-neuschwanstein-castle-archives

Teresa Nowakowski, "What Happened to the Treasure Nazis Buried in This Dutch Village?" May 9, 2023, accessed at https://www.smithsonianmag.com/smart-news/treasure-map-nazis-ommeren-180982137/

Stephanie Schoppert, "10 Pieces of Art Stolen by the Nazis that are Still Missing Today," History Collection, September 27, 2016, accessed at https://historycollection.com/10-pieces-art-stolen-nazis-still-missing-today/

Sky History UK, "The Amber Room: The World's Greatest Lost Treasure," accessed at "https://www.history.co.uk/article/the-mystery-of-the-amber-room-the-worlds-greatest-lost-treasure

Mindy Weisberger, "Nazi diary reveals secret location of WWII treasure under a palace in Poland," June 1, 2020, accessed at https://www.livescience.com/nazi-diary-buried-gold.html

Mitchell Willetts, "Cargo from Nazi ship sunk by America during WWII is washing up on Texas beaches," Fort Worth Star-Telegram, May 14, 2023, accessed at
https://www.star-telegram.com/news/state/texas/article275402851.html

The Death of Mr. Drum

Lesley Cowling, "Echoes of an African Drum: The Lost Literary Journalism of 1950s South Africa," *Literary Journalism Studies*, Vol. 8, No. 1, Spring 2016.

Clifton Crais and Thomas V. McClendon, *The South Africa Reader: History, Culture, and Politics*, The World Readers series, Duke University Press,

2014, available through JSTOR https://www.jstor.org/stable/j.ctv125jpdf

Anton Harber, "About Henry Nxumalo," Henry Nxumalo Foundation, 2022, accessed at https://henrynxumalofoundation.co.za/about-henry-nxumalo/

The Journalist Project, "Henry Nxumalo: A Courageous and Caring Father," October 29, 2014, accessed at https://www.thejournalist.org.za/pioneers/henry-nxumalo-courageous-caring-father/

The Journalist Project, "In Search of Mr. Drum: The daring Henry Nxumalo," October 1, 2014, accessed at https://www.thejournalist.org.za/pioneers/henry-nxumalo/

Mohamed Keita, "Remembering Henry Nxumalo, pioneer under apartheid," Committee to Protect Journalists, January 3, 2012, accessed at https://cpj.org/2012/01/remembering-henry-nxumalo-pioneer-under-apartheid/

Learn and Teach Foundation, "The man who made DRUM famous," originally published 1982, accessed at https://learnandteachmagazine.wordpress.com/2016/08/14/the-man-who-made-drum-famous/

South African History Online, "Drum Magazine," October 10, 2019, accessed at https://www.sahistory.org.za/article/drum-magazine

South African History Online, "Henry 'Mr Drum' Nxumalo," August 23, 2019, accessed at https://www.sahistory.org.za/people/henry-mr-drum-nxumalo

The Dead Mountain Ski Party

Rebecca Armitage, "The Dyatlov Pass incident sparked terror and conspiracy theories. But has the mystery finally been resolved?" accessed at https://www.abc.net.au/news/2022-06-25/dyatlov-pass-mystery-potentially-solved/101171704

Lucy Ash, "There were nine," BBC News, December 2019, https://www.bbc.co.uk/news/extra/SoLiOdJyCK/mystery_of_dyatlov_pass

Johan Gaume and Alexander M. Puzron, "Mechanisms of slab avalanche release and impact in the Dyatlov Pass incident in 1959," *Communications Earth & Environment*, 2021, accessed at https://www.nature.com/articles/s43247-020-00081-8

Teodora Hadjiyska and Igor Pavlov, *1079: The Overwhelming Force of Dyatlov Pass*, https://dyatlovpass.com/

Tim Newcomb, "How did Nine Hikers Die in the Dyatlov Pass Incident? New Evidence Teases the Truth," *Popular Mechanics*, February 6, 2023.

Douglas Preston, "Has an old Soviet mystery at last been solved?" *The New Yorker*, May 10, 2021, accessed at https://www.newyorker.com/magazine/2021/05/17/has-an-old-soviet-mystery-at-last-been-solved

Meilan Solly, "Have Scientists Finally Unraveled the 60-Year Mystery Surrounding Nine Russian Hikers' Deaths?" *Smithsonian Magazine*, January 29, 2021, accessed at https://www.smithsonianmag.com/smart-news/scientists-may-have-finally-unraveled-mystery-dyatlov-pass-incident-180976886/

The Fate of the Air Pirates

Associated Press, "American POWs sent to USSR, Yelstin says," June 16, 1992, accessed at https://www.deseret.com/1992/6/16/18989856/american-pows-sent-to-ussr-yeltsin-says/

Heather Atherton, "50 years later, peace treaty that was supposed to end Vietnam War still haunts my family," USA Today, February 2, 2023, accessed at https://www.usatoday.com/story/opinion/voices/2023/01/21/vietnam-war-paris-peace-accords-remember-baron-52/11021128002/

Mike Francis, "Still seeking answers about Joseph Matejov and many others missing in war," The Oregonian, January 11, 2014, accessed at https://www.oregonlive.com/pacific-northwest-news/2014/01/still_seeking_answers_about_jo.html

Library of Congress, A SERIES OF MEMORANDA CONCERNING BARON-52, 1994, Manuscript/Mixed Material, accessed at https://www.loc.gov/item/powmia/pwmaster_151021/.

Library of Congress, RESPONSE TO REFNOAND BARON-52, 1993, Manuscript/Mixed Material, accessed at https://www.loc.gov/item/powmia/pwmaster_151022/.

Library of Congress, RESPONSE TO REFNOAND BARON-52, 1993, Manuscript/Mixed Material, https://www.loc.gov/item/powmia/pwmaster_151022/.

Library of Congress, TECHNICAL CHARACTERISTICS OF EC-47Q BARON 52 REFNO, 1991, Manuscript/Mixed Material, accessed at https://www.loc.gov/item/powmia/pwmaster_151042/.

Library of Congress, SENATOR SMITH'S LETTER TO AMBASSADOR LORD

RE BARON 52, 1996, Manuscript/Mixed Material, accessed at https://www.loc.gov/item/powmia/pwmaster_154511/.

Library of Congress, OVERDUE AIRCRAFT, BARON-52 IS OVERDUE. WITH RELATED MESSAGES, 1973, Manuscript/Mixed Material, accessed at https://www.loc.gov/item/powmia/pwmaster_151046/.

Library of Congress, ANALYST NOTES, SUBJECT: LOSS OF BARON 52 AND CREW, 5 FEBRUARY, 1987, Manuscript/Mixed Material, accessed at https://www.loc.gov/item/powmia/pwmaster_65804/.

Library of Congress, FAMILY CONFERENCE REPORT, 1996, Manuscript/Mixed Material, accessed at https://www.loc.gov/item/powmia/pwmaster_151013/.

Thomas W. Lippman, "U.S. Team to Inspect Possible POW Prison in Laos," The Washington Post, January 15, 1994, accessed at https://www.washingtonpost.com/archive/politics/1994/01/16/us-team-to-inspect-possible-pow-prison-in-laos/c9f4690e-1c2d-4eb9-a417-8052f7f67a48/

Mark Millican, "Vietnam vet's 1973 disappearance still a mystery but puzzle of his bracelet solved," Dalton Daily Citizen, September 15, 2023, accessed at https://www.dailycitizen.news/news/local_news/vietnam-vet-s-1973-disappearance-still-a-mystery-but-puzzle-of-his-bracelet-solved/article_99875e50-4735-11ee-a1cf-ffeca078dffb.html

James C. Wheeler, "Unarmed, Alone, and Afraid," EC-47 History Site, accessed at https://www.ec47.com/unarmed-alone-and-afraid

Will the real thieves please raise Perón's hand?

Shirley Christian, "Perón Hands: Police Find Trail Elusive," The New York Times, September 6, 1987, accessed at https://www.nytimes.-com/1987/09/06/world/Perón-hands-police-find-trail-elusive.html

Linda Pressly, "The 20-year odyssey of Eva Perón's body," BBC News, July 26, 2012, accessed at https://www.bbc.com/news/magazine-18616380

Reuter, "Thieves Ask $8 Million for Hands of Perón," July 2, 1987, available at https://www.washingtonpost.com/archive/politics/1987/07/03/thieves-ask-8-million-for-hands-of-Perón/db533d40-2d92-43e6-a433-ab345f708db8/

Guillermo dos Santos Coelho, "El día que robaron las manos de Perón," Clarin, June 29, 2017, accessed at

https://www.clarin.com/especiales/dia-robaron-manos-Perón_0_rJ4qoHWVW.html

Sergio Sarachu, "Fue macabro: entraron a la tumba y robaron las manos de Perón," Alerta Digital, June 29, 2023, accessed at
https://alertadigital.ar/fue-macabro-entraron-a-la-tumba-y-robaron-las-manos-de-Perón/

Alden Whitman, "Perón, After Years as Strongman, Arose From Defeat to Rule Argentina Again," The New York Times, July 2, 1974, accessed at https://www.nytimes.com/1974/07/02/archives/Perón-after-years-as-strongman-arose-from-defeat-to-rule-argentina.html

Tank Man

Amnesty International, "What really happened in the 1989 Tiananmen Square protests," May 18, 2023, accessed at https://www.amnesty.org.uk/china-1989-tiananmen-square-protests-demonstration-massacre

BBC News, "Tiananmen Square Tank Man photographer Charlie Cole dies," September 12, 2019, accessed at https://www.bbc.com/news/world-asia-china-49684808

Gordon Corera, "The escaped dissident still pursued decades on by China," BBC News, May 11, 2024, accessed at https://www.bbc.com/news/articles/crgy7xypwj8o

Krysta Fauria And Christopher Bodeen, "'Tank man' photographer urges China to open up on Tiananmen," AP News, June 1, 2019, accessed at https://apnews.com/article/31d22de9e1b14322adf2457d11e4891f

Julie Makinen, Tiananmen Square mystery: Who was 'Tank Man'?" Los Angeles Times, June 4, 2014, accessed at https://www.latimes.com/world/asia/la-fg-china-tiananmen-square-tank-man-20140603-story.html

Kate Pickert, "Tank Man at 25: Behind the Iconic Tiananmen Square Photo," Time, June 4, 2014, accessed at https://time.com/2822322/iconic-tiananmen-tank-man-photo/

Michael Ray, "Tank Man," Britannica, September 14, 2024, accessed at https://www.britannica.com/biography/Tank-Man

Patrick Witty, "Tank Man Revisited: More Details Emerge About the Iconic Image," Time, June 5, 2012, accessed at https://time.com/3788986/tiananmen/

Unidentified Flying Objects

Rae Alexandra, "In 1896, a Mysterious UFO Brought Northern California to a Mesmerized Halt," KQED, accessed at

https://www.kqed.org/arts/13957514/1896-mystery-airship-bay-area-ufo-history-victorian-aliens

Nuray Bulbul, "Pentagon reveals Japan as UFO sighting hotspot," The Standard, September 5, 2023, accessed at

https://www.standard.co.uk/news/world/pentagon-japan-ufo-sighting-hotspot-b1104973.html

Jacquelyn DiNick, "Navy pilots recall 'unsettling' 2004 UAP sighting," CBS News: 60 Minutes Overtime, May 16, 2021, accessed at https://www.cbsnews.com/news/navy-ufo-sighting-60-minutes-2021-05-16/

George Knapp, "Las Vegas Based Scientists Study 'Skinwalker Ranch,'" Internet Archive, December 21, 2005 accessed at https://web.archive.org/web/20070927223735/http://www.klas-tv.com/Global/story.asp?S=4275629

Desiree Kocis, "Ghost Airships of the 1800s," *Plane & Pilot*, April 6, 2020, accessed at https://www.planeandpilotmag.com/article/ghost-airships-of-the-1800s/

Woody LaBounty, "1896 UFO," San Francisco Story, November 22, 2023, accessed at https://www.sanfranciscostory.com/1896-ufo/

Las Vegas Sun, "Nevada Millionaire Buys 'UFO Ranch' in Utah," October 23, 1996, accessed at https://lasvegassun.com/news/1996/oct/23/nevada-millionaire-buys-ufo-ranch-in-utah/

Russell Lee, "1947: Year of the Flying Saucer," National Air and Space Museum, June 24, 2022, accessed at https://airandspace.si.edu/stories/editorial/1947-year-flying-saucer

Michael Mitsanas, "Here are the 5 most memorable moments from Congress' UFO hearing," NBC News, July 26, 2023, accessed at

https://www.nbcnews.com/politics/congress/are-5-memorable-moments-congress-ufo-hearing-rcna96476

Richard Padula, "The day UFOs stopped to play," BBC News, October 24, 2014, accessed at https://www.bbc.com/news/magazine-29342407

The San Fransisco Call and Post, "Saw the Mystic Flying Light," November 22, 1896, accessed at https://www.newspapers.com/article/the-san-francisco-call-and-post-1896-ufo/38656678/

Christine Steinuehler, "Airship Alert!" *KANSAS! Magazine*, June 16, 2022, accessed at https://www.travelks.com/kansas-magazine/articles/post/airship-alert/

Travis Tritten, "How Believers in the Paranormal Birthed the Pentagon's New Hunt for UFOs," Military.com, March 7, 2022, accessed at https://www.military.com/daily-news/2022/03/07/how-believers-paranormal-birthed-pentagons-new-hunt-ufos.html

Stefanie Waldek, "History's Most Infamous UFO Sightings of the Modern Era," History, December 8, 2020, accessed at https://www.history.com/news/historys-most-infamous-ufo-sightings

Mike Wendling, "US says UFO sighting likely secret military tests," BBC News, March 8, 2020, accessed at https://www.bbc.com/news/uk-68515515

Epilogue: The Somerton Man

Sara Garcia, "What do we know about Carl Webb? Researchers find ads, photographs to paint picture of well-to-do man," ABC News, September 7, 2022, accessed at https://www.abc.net.au/news/2022-09-08/somerton-man-found-in-nephews-clothe-researchers-believes/101405152

Meilan Solly, "Have Scholars Finally Identifed the Mysterious Somerton Man?" Smithsonian Magazine, August 8, 2022, accessed at https://www.smithsonianmag.com/smart-news/have-scholars-finally-identified-the-mysterious-somerton-man-180980540/

ALSO BY E.B. WHEELER

British Fiction:

Born to Treason

The Royalist's Daughter

The Haunting of Springett Hall

Wishwood (Westwood Gothic)

Moon Hollow (Westwood Gothic)

A Proper Dragon (Dragons of Mayfair 1)

An Elusive Dragon (Dragons of Mayfair 2)

A Subtle Dragon (Dragons of Mayfair 3)

Cruel Magic (Iron & Thorns 1)

Wild Magic (Iron & Thorns 2)

Fierce Magic (Iron & Thorns 3)

A Haunted Masquerade (A Haunted Season)

Utah Fiction:

No Peace with the Dawn (with Jeffery Bateman)

Letters from the Homefront (Utah at War)

Balm for the Heart (Utah at War)

Bootleggers and Basil (in *The Pathways to the Heart*)

Blood in a Dry Town (Tenny Mateo Mystery 1)

A Company of Bones (Tenny Mateo Mystery 2)

Nonfiction:

Utah Women: Pioneers, Poets & Politicians

Mysteries of the Old West

Mysteries of the Middle Ages

Juvenile Fiction:

The Bone Map

Alejandra the Axolotl and the Big Mess

ACKNOWLEDGMENTS

Thank you to my critique group The Writers' Cache and to my beta readers, Alex, Dan, Karen, and Keri for their feedback and taking some of the mystery out of writing. And as always, I couldn't do this without the understanding, patience, and support of my family and especially my husband.

Links to Creative Commons image licenses:

GNU 2.5 (https://www.gnu.org/licenses/old-licenses/gpl-2.0.html)

CC BY 2.0 (https://creativecommons.org/licenses/by/2.0/)

CC BY-SA 2.0 (https://creativecommons.org/licenses/by-sa/2.0/)

CC BY-SA 3.0 (https://creativecommons.org/licenses/by-sa/3.0/)

CC BY 4.0 (https://creativecommons.org/licenses/by/4.0/)

CC BY-SA 4.0 (https://creativecommons.org/licenses/by-sa/4.0/)

ABOUT THE AUTHOR

E.B. Wheeler attended BYU, majoring in history with an English minor, and earned graduate degrees in history and landscape architecture from Utah State University. She's the author of over a dozen books, including *The Bone Map*, *Utah Women: Pioneers, Poets & Politicians,* and Whitney Award winner *Cruel Magic,* as well as several short stories, magazine articles, and scripts for educational programs. The League of Utah Writers named her the Writer of the Year in 2016. In addition to writing, she consults about historic preservation and teaches history.

www.ingramcontent.com/pod-product-compliance
Lightning Source LLC
Chambersburg PA
CBHW060226030426
42335CB00014B/1349

* 9 7 8 1 9 6 0 0 3 3 1 5 4 *